PEACE RIVER

A CANOE VOYAGE FROM
HUDSON'S BAY TO PACIFIC

PEACE RIVER

A CANOE VOYAGE FROM HUDSON'S BAY TO PACIFIC

BY

SIR GEORGE SIMPSON

(Governor, Hon. Hudson's Bay Company.)

IN 1828

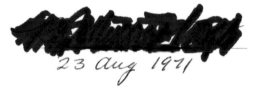

23 Aug 1971

JOURNAL

Of the late Chief Factor, Archibald McDonald (Hon. Hudson's Bay Company), who accompanied him.

~~~~~~~~~

EDITED, WITH NOTES,
BY
MALCOLM McLEOD.
BARRISTER, ETC.

~~~~~~~~~

M. G. HURTIG LTD.
Booksellers & Publishers
EDMONTON

PRINTED IN JAPAN

Introduction to the New Edition

In the days of the fur trade in what is now Western Canada, the great entrepôt of trade goods from Europe was York Factory on Hudson Bay. The goods were shipped inland by canoe along the various waterways to the trading posts in the interior and to posts over the Rockies on the Pacific slope. This book describes a canoe voyage along the longest of the routes, from York Factory to Fort Langley near the mouth of the Fraser River, a distance of some 3,200 miles. The journey by Governor Simpson and his party, travelling without freight, occupied nearly three months, but two weeks of this were spent in business at posts along the way. Were the reader to attempt to retrace the route by canoe today, he would find many of the waterways much as they were in Simpson's day, largely traversing wilderness or thinly settled areas. Recently constructed dams in Manitoba and British Columbia will, however, have drowned miles of the original river bed.

A reissue of Archibald McDonald's journal of the voyage would seem to be in no need of a further introduction, since Malcolm McLeod, the editor of the original, provided an introduction of nineteen pages, including the itinerary in tabular form for quick reference. Moreover, McLeod's appendices of seventy-two notes are twice as long as the thirty-nine-page journal. The excuse then for a further introduction to *Peace River* is to provide biographical information on Archibald McDonald, the fur-trade diarist, and on his editor, Malcolm McLeod. The reader may also wish to know the significance of the first appearance in print of the journal in 1872, forty-four years after it was written.

The author, Archibald McDonald, first came to Rupert's Land in 1813 as leader of a party of Lord Selkirk's colonists. Under Governor Miles Macdonell, he served as deputy governor of the Red River Settlement, and was a participant in the dispute between the colonists and the North West Company. He wrote two pamphlets relating to the Red River troubles which were published in Montreal in 1816. The first was entitled *Narrative respecting the destruction of the Earl of Selkirk's settlement upon the Red River in 1815;* the second was his *Reply to the letter lately addressed to the Earl of Selkirk by the Hon. and Rev. John Strachan.*

McDonald entered the service of the Hudson's Bay Company, and after the union with the rival North West Company in 1821, was sent to the Columbia River on the Pacific coast. The year of the canoe journey, 1828, he was promoted to chief trader and, until 1833, was in charge of Fort Langley. From 1834 until 1844 he was in command of Fort Colvile and became a chief factor. After his retirement he settled at St. Andrew's in Lower Canada, where he died on January 15th, 1853, shortly before his sixty-third birthday.

McDonald was twice married and had a number of children. His first wife, a daughter of Chief Com-Comly of the Chinook tribe, died shortly after giving birth to a son, Ranald. As a young man Ranald spent the year 1848–49 in Japan, one of the first foreigners to visit the hermit nation prior to Commodore Perry's Treaty of 1854 which opened Japan to outside commerce.

When visiting in Canada in 1853 Ranald left the notes of his Japanese adventure with Malcolm McLeod who, over a period of more than thirty years, sought to have the account published as a book. Finally, in 1923, twenty-nine years after Ranald's death, the book was published by the Eastern Washington Historical Society in Spokane, Washington.

Now, a note about Malcolm McLeod, editor and literary executor of the papers of the McDonalds, father and son. McLeod was born in 1821 at Green Lake, Beaver River, in Rupert's Land, the son of a Hudson's Bay Company factor. He was educated in Edinburgh and in Montreal where he studied law. From 1845 he practiced law in Lower Canada, and for a short time was a district judge. He died in Ottawa in 1899. He is remembered as the author of a number of pamphlets on the Pacific railway and possible routes.

Editor McLeod had a purpose when he published this volume in 1872. Three years earlier, the new Dominion of Canada had purchased Rupert's Land from the Hudson's Bay Company and at this time was engaging surveyors, geologists and botanists to appraise the potentiality of the vast territories lying west of the Great Lakes. Moreover, in the previous year, 1871, British Columbia had entered Confederation on condition that a railway be constructed across Rupert's Land to the Pacific. For the next dozen years the route of the railway would be the subject of much public debate and many surveys.

In McDonald's journal, Malcolm McLeod saw an opportunity to influence Canadian public opinion. He wished to bring attention to the agricultural possibilities of the forest belt stretching to the Arctic Circle, and in particular to that area drained by the Peace River. His second purpose was to draw attention to the Peace River Pass as one of the best routes through the Rocky Mountains for any railway or wagon road. A book, therefore, that should more properly have been called by its subtitle, *A Canoe Voyage from Hudson's Bay to Pacific*, became, at a crucial time in Canadian history, *Peace River*.

BRUCE PEEL

University of Alberta
October 1969

PREFACE.

——:o:——

The object of the present *brochure*, at this juncture, is to direct attention—by an account of a canoe voyage through the region—to the fact that *beyond* that "*Belt*" of *supposed limited* fertility, which is implied in the term "Fertile Belt," there is, in our North West, an area, continuous in every direction and easily accessible to its utmost limits, containing *over three hundred millions* of acres of wheat and pasture lands, with forests of finest timber, and the largest known coal and bitumen, and also probably richest gold areas in the world—a land teeming with animal and vegetable life, extending to the very Arctic Circle, and owing its wealth in that respect to *exceptional* causes. I refer to that area—comprised entirely of Silurian and Devonian systems—watered by the great Athabasca, Peace, and McKenzie Rivers, with their countless affluents.

Another fact, to which, I think it necessary to direct attention is, that the great and beautiful and *fertile* Plateau of Middle and even of much of Northern British Columbia, is not too high, nor too cold, nor objectionable on any score for settlement, especially to Canadians accustomed to contend with frost and snow in the measure to be there found.

This subject is comparatively untouched, because unknown, by publicists, and I flatter myself that my fellow Canadians will appreciate such a country for *them*, inasmuch as they can best deal with it. In the opened, and still further opening gold fields in and about that upper region, there is, and there must ever be, from its comparative isolation, an excellent local market for the farmer : and, moreover, the coast, with its large population and its mining as well as fishing industries, would furnish a large and good market.

Thirdly,—and it is to this particular fact, as a present objective point, that I would respectfully call attention :

The lowest, easiest and best PASS of the Rocky Mountains, in fact the *only* one which presents—say by such a Territorial Trunk Road, as Mr. Fleming in his Memorial to the Imperial and Canadian Governments, proposed in 1863—a practical gateway to the Pacific Slope, to the waggon of the settler, is the Peace River Pass, and which is less—I make it— than eighteen hundred feet above the sea.

Governor Simpson in his bark canoe—the very one he had, a few days before, embarked in at York Factory, Hudson's Bay—paddled through it, on its from a quarter to half a mile in breadth of lacrustine water-course, with all the ease of a " paddle on a quiet lake."

The Journal I now give, with accompanying explanatory notes, is the account of that remarkable trip. I call it a Journal, but evidently it was a mere memorandum, for private keeing, of facts and incidents along the way, and was never intended for publication.

The Widow and legal representatives of my lamented friend the late Chief Factor A. McDonald have, with a public spirit which commends itself, allowed me the use of his " Notes," as he calls them—They are now given as called for—That they are so *crudely* given is my fault ; and I have but to trust to the generosity of those who may honor the little work with a reading, pleading as my excuse, that the call on me for the effort was only the other day made, and that it has only been at snatched moments from engrossing business duties, and at odd hours in the night, that I have been able thus, with running pen, to throw off these hurried pages, to meet what seems a pressing call and enquiry.

                                                              M. M.

Aylmer, County of Ottawa,

                              May, 1872.

P.S. The words within brackets, in the narrative, are by the Editor, in explanation.

ADDENDUM.

———:o:———

Since these pages were put in press, I have had the pleasure of reading the Honorable Mr. Langevin's exhaustive and very valuable Report of British Columbia. It touches on all subjects in or about the country, and he has drawn information, evidently, from every possible source at his command, and of course, he has done so with that care which is due to the character of his work.

In the mass and multiplicity of subjects on which the information is given, I am glad to be able to say, that in no instance has any statement of mine, nor even any estimate on the few rude materials I had to work on, viz., old fur trade reports, and personal incidents of nearly half a century ago, been contradicted, or shown to be, in the slightest degree, untrue or wrong. In other words, speaking from totally different stand points, we but corroborate each other.

There is one point, however, on which, I feel, that I ought to have spoken more fully, and as to which, my partial reticence may cause a wrong impression. It is as to the climate of the country.

On this head, I have confined my remarks to the region covered, through a course of years, by the Harmon Journal, cited in one or more of my notes in Appendix. The observations, there, indicate a climate of almost average Canadian severity. Such, I believe, is the case in that *upper*, yea, I may say *uppermost* region of British Columbia, namely, the great plateau extending northwards from the upper great bend of the Fraser,

South of that—say between Cariboo and Kamloops—the winter is certainly much milder. From a letter in my possession from the officer (one George McDougall) in charge of Fort Alexander (the most northerly post then in that area) letter dated 8th March, 1828, I believe that it was *unusual* for the Lakes to remain frozen to that date, and that the continuance of snow and ice there to that time marked the winter as one of unusual severity : at the same time however, the letter says, that the horses had, in the open, " stood it out well," and were in good condition. The letter was addressed to my father. Amongst my father's papers, I find also, that on *17th February*, 1826, the route being then free of snow, he started, *with horses*, to travel over hundreds of miles of mountain trail to the mouth of the Okanagan.

My own personal recollections as to Kamloops and the country about it, associate it with heat and sunshine, and scarcely, if at all, with snow or bad weather.

There is also another subject on which I could only make a general statement, and that, only conjecturally, I may say, for my information on the subject (a private letter to myself) was not such as I could well use, without special permission. It is as to the new gold mining district, known as the *Omenica Mines* (gold and silver) and in which is " *Germansen Creek*," whereof a report, of some length and importance, is given in Mr. Langevin's work. Germansen Creek is within a couple of days' paddle, (so I estimate) of the Peace River Pass. Sir George, in his canoe, might have floated into it, and even beyond, but how far, I cannot say. From the Pass to the head of steamboat navigation on the Skeena, is only about 350 miles altogether, and the route is, I believe, comparatively easy.

*   *   *   *   *   *

MR. FLEMING'S CANADIAN PACIFIC RAILWAY SURVEY REPORT.

Since beginning to correct the proof sheets of this pamphlet, I have been favored with a copy of Mr. Fleming's " Progress Report of Canadian Pacific Railway Survey."

I am glad to see that it does not clash with any statement of mine as to altitude, distance, or physical features of route in question, nor, in fact, as to anything I have ever written on the subject. But it is not to say this, that I would allude to it, but to give my humble testimony to the special character of some of the service done in that work. I allude to the great feat—for that is what it really is—of Mr. R. McLennan and his party in penetrating the wood choked, boggy, and glacier covered mountain fastnesses of the head waters of the North Thompson. It is a region which has hitherto been impenetrable, even, I believe, to the Indian. I see, amongst my father's reports to the Governor and Council of the Hudson's Bay Company in 1823, when he was in charge of the Thompson's River District, which embraced the region in question, that up to that time his predecessors—and among them were men of keen intelligence and great energy, and especially Chief Factor Peter Skene Ogden (brother of the late Charles Ogden, Attorney General of Lower Canada, and afterwards Chief Justice of the Isle of Man)—had failed in every effort to even enter that region, for trade. My father had a plan for the purpose, which appeared likely to succeed, if tried, but as it involved some risk and cost it had first to be approved by the authorities, and there, I believe, the matter dropt.

McLennan did well, but the work at this *hinging point* for railway route to the Pacific, has yet to be completed by a survey of the few miles, about fifteen only, I believe, between Albreda Lake (where a winter party is at work) and the Quesnel watershed. [Note by Editor. The survey has been since completed, and a practicable route *there*, for railway, found as I predicted in my letter seven of the " Britannicus " Series of 1869, defining a practicable Pacific Railway Route.]

As to the other " difficult part " of the route, viz., that north of Lake Superior, I, in common with all Hudson's Bay people, always knew that a railroad along the north shore of Lake Superior was impossible, but that some distance back, say 150 or 160 miles, and the further back the better, there is, along the plateau " height of land " which is the rim of the great basin (silurian) of Hudson's Bay, fine level ground for a railway.

I, some time ago, pointed to the north end of Long Lake, which is a little north of Nipegon, as an objective point. At the same time, I presume, that as the survey has to be an exhaustive one, the *impossibility* of certain lines of route, such as the one to touch the north shore of Lake Superior, and the one across the Rocky Mountains by the Howse Pass, and thence through the " Eagle Pass " of the " Snowy Mountains " to the Shuswhap Lakes of the Thompson, has to be determined. As to what has been done on the survey for our Pacific Railway, there can, in reason, be but one opinion, viz., that it has been conceived and ordered throughout, in its immense and novel detail, with consummate skill, and urged with unparalleled energy on the part of all engaged, and the Government and its staff in the work deserve all credit. What the Americans took about *ten years* to do, we, with really greater difficulties to cope with, have done—and well done, so far—in ten *months,* or less !

But it is not only a railroad to the Pacific that we want, but, more still, perhaps, or at least equally so, a *Roadway for Immigrant Waggons* —large household waggons that will carry, at one lift, a farmer's whole "belongings," from the Railway Car at Pembina or Winnipeg, to Pacific Omenica, through the Peace River Pass. At every halting place, at every step, in that truly golden way—a stretch of almost continuously level sward fifteen hundred miles in length—nature, all bountiful, has, in a manner, strewed her manna, and abundance is *there, all along,* for man, and for the animals that serve him. I say waggons, but the indestructible " Red River Cart " might answer at the start. In any case, a regular Transport Service, with European agencies for " *through* tickets " (clinching in Europe for *Canada*) would have to be organized, and for a large and general immigration, a subsidized chartered body, under direct Governmental superintendence, if not control, working at certain fixed rates, and under effectual guarantee of fidelity to the service as one of public moment, suggests itself. For the present, I forbear from saying any more on this subject, satisfied that there are other minds more potential, working in the direction indicated.

M. M.

ITINERARY.—CANOE COURSE.

Place.	Date. A.D. 1828.	Remarks.	Distance. Statute Miles.	Aggregates.
Hudson's Bay.				
York Factory	July 12— 1 a.m.	"Started against Tide."		
Norway House	,, 19— 7 p.m.	Arrived. For details of route see Journal and Note XII. of Appendix.	430	430
	,, 20—11 a.m.	Started.		
"Warren's Point"	,, 20— 4 p.m.	Arrived. Windbound.	20	
	,, 21— 4 a.m.	Wind a little ahead all day.		
First Lime Stone Point	,, 21—Evening	Wind ahead.		
Mouth of Saskatchewan	,, 22— 9 a.m.	Remained an hour, drying things. Mounted Upper Rapids.	90	
Head of Grand Rapid	,, 22— 3 p.m.	Got over Cross Lake, and camped at head of Cross Lake Rapid.		
Head of Cross Lake Rapid	,, 23— 2 a.m.	Started.		
Cumberland House	,, 26— 2 p.m.	Arrived.	190	730
Rivière Maligne	,, 27— 3½ a.m.	Started. Lake, and water in river tolerably good.	60	
About 16 miles above Island and Pine Portage	,, 28—Noon	"Good water." Several strong rapids. Stretch of still water.	55	
	,, 29— 2 a.m.	"Good water." Island and Pine Portages took two hours; Pelican Lake, 2 hours; from 11 to 12, three short portages; then Portage des Bois—Lake des Bois, seven hours (Frog Portage).	60	
Frog Portage	,, 30— 3 a.m.	From Lower end. Breakfast at head of first Grand Rapid in English River.	50	
	,, 31— 3 a.m.	Many rapids, some very steep; portages, but with lakes and comparatively still water at intervals .....Say	200	
	Aug. 1— 2½ a.m.			
	,, 2— 2 a.m.			
	,, 3— 2 a.m.			
Fort of Lac de l'Ile à la Crosse	,, 4—11 a.m.	Arrived.		1,155
	,, 5— 3½ a.m.	Started.		
Methy Portage (lower end)	,, 7—Evening	(Called also Portage La Loche). Arrived; passage nearly all lake, and easy. [See Notes XXVIII., XXX., and XXXIV. in Appendix].	130	
Head of Portage	,, 8— 4 p.m.	Assisted by Indians; carried all in one trip.	12	1,297

ITINERARY.—CANOE COURSE.—*Continued.*

Place.	Date. A.D. 1828.	Remarks.	Distance. Statute Miles.	Aggregates.
White Mud Portage	Aug. 8 — 7 p.m.	Left head of Methy Portage at ¼ to 5 p.m., and "made" the White Mud Portage by 7 p.m.	15	
"	9 — 4 a.m.	Started	80	
"	9 — 5 p.m.	Passed mouth of Pembina River	11	
Six miles from mouth of Clear W. R.	10 — 4 a.m.	Encamped late, within a couple of leagues of Athabasca River. Started. Water shoal	75	
	10 — 10½ a.m.	Red River, and little hills opposite		
	10 — About noon	Passed *Bituminous Springs*		
	10 — 2 p.m.	*Pierre au Calumet*, (old Fort)		
	10 — Evening	Camped at Poplar Point. "Large strata of pit coal all along either side of the river." See Note XXXVIII. in Appendix.		1,538
Fort Chipewyan	11 — 7 p.m.	Arrived	60	
"	14 — Noon	Started		
Mountain Falls	18 — 8 a.m.	Arrived, and passed on at say 11 a.m	220	
Fort Vermilion	20 — 10 a.m.	Current increasing	100	
"	22 — 6 a.m.	Started		
Cadotte's River	25	Encamped at Spring Islands, near Mr. Colin Campbell's house. "River seems here imbedded in sandstone rock, which shows on both sides." "*Sandstone emitting large* COLUMNS OF BLACK EARTH on the hills, from above the margin of the rock." See Note XLIX. in Appendix.	250	2,108
Dunvegan	27 — Sunset	Arrived. Increased current. See Note LIII. in Appendix.		
"	29 — 6 a.m.	Started. No mention of currents. Encamped early, below "the Islands without name"	30	
	30 — Say 5 a.m.	"Made an early start." "*Strong current all day.*" (See Note LIV. in Appendix.) "Great appearance of beaver." "Encamped at *La Grève,* near the river"	25	
	31 — Say 5 a.m.	"Breakfasted on Pemican Island, and dined about 500 yards below Fort d'Epinette," near the same distance above it is *Fort d'Epinette.* Encamped within a short distance of Mr. Yale's house, on left hand. Did not land at St. John's, where the people were murdered	30	2,193

Locality	Date	Time	Remarks	Dist.	Elev.
Old Mountain House, called also Rocky Mountain House, foot of Portage at the Bend	Sept.	1— 5 a.m.	"Passed Grande Fourche," i.e., Forks of "Grand River," a southern affluent, probably Sinew River. "Current Strong," ... Before breakfast passed another "Grande Fourche" on right. Above Rivière Maligne at noon. Dined at Les Isles de Pierre. "Soon after, had a glance of the Rocky Mountains, a few leagues off."	25	2,248
	,,	2— 5 a.m.	See Note LVIII. in Appendix. "Current not so strong to-day."	30	
	,,	2— 5 p.m.	"Arrived at portage at 5. Immediately, eight men, with the two canoes, proceeded by water, probably to examine the river (for they did not actually start till next morning), while with the remaining ten we made the portage. Incamped on the first fine level above the water, opposite Old Mountain House, which is on the south side." "Near where we landed the rocks, in several places, poured out spouts of clear water, as if coming from the mouth of a gun."		
Upper end of Bend	,,	4—Evening	Not so stated in Journal, but it must have been so, for next morning the canoe men walked from head of portage and met the land party. Distance from foot to head of Bend by water......	35	
Head of Portage	,,	5—	Portage, according to Journal, 9½ miles, including one part called the "Worst Road in Christendom," being, in fact, no road at all, and up "banks;" no hill or other uprise than the "upper bank," at the start as mentioned. The rest of the route is represented as being level, "tolerably clear," with one small swamp, and creek on the way.		
,,	,,	6— 3 a.m.	Started "with the line." First "line" on this river in present voyage, and the "last," at least so far as appears from journal. Long day's work. "Line" continued, except when we could not help it, till breakfast time. Dined at Pointe des Grèves de la Grande Prairie. Incamped about two leagues above the two rivers, which were passed at "half-past four"......	40	2,343
,,	,,	7— 3¾ a.m.	Passed Belair's River on right at 9. Mounted the Grand Rapid at 9, and breakfasted. Clear Water R. on left at 11; Round Island, 1 p.m.; Hill's Gate (or Hell Gate) on right about 5. ...... "THE MOUNTAINS THIS AFTERNOON ASSUME A STUPENDOUS APPEARANCE." See Note LVIII. in Appendix. Encarped at Bernard's River......	30	
Pass of the Mountains	,,			10	
Bernard's River, 10 miles beyond Pass	Sept.	8—Started late. Say 4 a.m.	At another Grand Rapid by 7, and at Finlay's Branch 20 minutes after.	10	2,363
Finlay's Branch	,,	8— 7·20 a.m.	Little Forks, i.e., on Peace River, by tributary from westward.	12	
Peace River (i.e., the south branch)	,,	8—11 a.m.	No word of current, rapids, but only of "fine dry beaches," and easy going......	20	

ITINERARY.—CANOE VOYAGE.—*Continued.*

Place.	Date. A.D. 1828.	Remarks.	Distance. Statute Miles.	Aggregates.
	Sept. 9—Probably 3½ a.m.	Fine day. Breakfasted at 9. At La Prairie by 1. *River le Mouton* (or some such word) at 3, and *Le Grand Remou* before sunset. Encamped about a league above. Evidently good and easy water. Saw a number of geese. River probably lacustrine....	45	
	,, 10—Probably 3½ a.m.	Passed *Pointe La Loche* at 7 a.m. Peace River diminishing fast; left it and entered Black Water Creek at 3. Encamped at entrance of Lac La Loche very late....	40	2,495
	,, 11—Early—3 a.m.	"Lake took us half an hour this morning; entered little river by right hand. Breakfasted about 200 yards from, and just before we entered Trout or McLeod's Lake." Entered Lake and Fort.	15	
McLeod's Fort......	,, 13— 5 a.m.	"Started on foot, every man with a load. Arrived at first lake before 7, at 2nd by 8½; breakfasted; off again by 11; reached Long Lake about 4; last half of the way very very bad; plenty of water all along," "Distance, 18 miles"....	18	
,, 18th Mile Campment..	,, 14—Daylight.....	Started. "Long Lake took us an hour" (going along it, probably); to Round Lake, another; and by 8 were at east side of Carp Lake. Traverse of lake took us three hours, on a very frail raft. Resumed journey at 4. At Small Lake at 6. On our right is what is called the *Brulé*. Total distance to-day....	15	
,, 33rd Mile......	,, 15—Daylight.....	Arrived at River La Cache in an hour and a half, and at Half-way Creek in about same time. Came a short way further, and breakfasted at the edge of a small lake to the left. Encamped on a small prairie. Point of woods took us two hours, and from there to White River half as long, over *very fine country*. Rest of day, two hours more. Encamped at 4 p.m. Total....	20	
,, 53rd Mile...... 53rd Mile......	Sept. 16— 6 a.m......	Good walking in the morning. Left *Lac des Morts*, and another small one on left hand, and arrived at Carrier Lake to breakfast. Crossed small inlet in Carrier Lake, which took an hour. Encamped within 12 miles of the Fort. Total....	18	
,, 71st Mile...... ,, 83rd Mile....	,, 17—......	Started late. Horses (4) met on the way, having strayed. Halted for breakfast at last lake before arriving at the Fort, within a mile of it. Entered Fort St. James.......	12	

Place	Date	Notes	Miles	Altitude
Fort St. James.........	Sept. 17—2 p.m.	[See Notes LXIII., LXIV., LXV. in Appendix..........	......	2,578
,,	24—Noon........	Roy arrived with the canoes, and in 25 minutes we were off. In a quarter of an hour we reached the river (Stuart River), outlet of Lake Stuart). Made eight leagues.	24	
,,	25—Before daylight	In still water till 5. Breakfasted at head of rapids, eight miles above the Small Forks, formed by junction of Fraser's River, *i.e.*, western branch of Fraser's River. "Encamped at 6, about an hour's march above the main forks. Fine navigation all day."		
,,	26..............	At Grand Forks (of Fraser River, from the east) at 5. West Road River (Sir Alexander McKenzie's route to Ocean to Bentinck Arm) at 11. *River des Liards*, on left, at 4; and a few minutes after, the *Clay Pyramids* on each side. Quesnel's River at 5½ p.m. Encamped three miles lower down....	70	
Fort Alexander (called also Alexandria).........	,, 27—10 a.m.	Canoes waited here for the Land Party. Encamped at 5. Strong head wind, preventing progress. Camp stated at only.....	90 / 30	2,782
FORKS of Fraser and Thompson Rivers (now Lytton)	Oct. 8— 1 p.m.	Started with the miserable Thompson River boat, and the two bark canoes, to *run the Fraser River Canon*, which not one of the party had gone through nor seen, and which had never, so far as known, been run before by any one. "Governor embarked with me (Macdonald) in the boat. Off, when we could well see in the *dalles*. Were soon in a long rapid, with a small stream from the mountains on right hand, at foot. Good run to Allitza River, on the same side, which we passed at 8, leaving the other about half way. *Strong whirlpools* below, which forced Bernard to return and descend on the opposite side. From this place (where we were detained three-quarters of an hour) we had a good run over a current of *great velocity*, to the *Rivière de Sable* ("Sandy River"), which we made about 9, and breakfasted. Gummed, and ran dalles till 12. "*This is a bad piece of navigation.*" Five hundred yards lower down, made use of our lines, and at the foot of the same cascade, on right hand, carried the canoes; and here we were detained, repairing, gumming, &c., for two hours. The *boat ran the portage part of the river*, but required great skill and vigilance. The boat had a peep at the next place before the canoes came on. This place we call the Gate Dalles. Very good going down, but should a line be required to ascend, it will be a task of some difficulty to pass it on either side. First rapid, of another nature (not easy), at 3; then a smooth piece of a few miles before we came to Mr. Yale's River, which has also a strong rapid at its mouth, and to get down, the guide was "induced" to land the passengers and two men out of each canoe. There was some delay before they could ford the river."—[Note	250	
	,, 9— 6 a.m..........		4	

ITINERARY.—CANOE VOYAGE.—*Continued.*

Place.	Date, A.D. 1828.	Remarks.	Distance. Statute Miles.	Aggregates.
		by Editor: These cross-waters are ever most uncontrollable and dangerous, the under currents especially being out of ken and calculation, and often of most treacherous working.]—"Left this place at 4, and in 20 minutes arrived at the HEAD OF THE FALL. Examined it minutely. *Boat undertook to run right down mid-channel*; did so, keeping rather in eddy to the right, and did not ship more than we had, on one or two occasions, already experienced. The canoes crossed to the west side, and made a portage over a good sandy beach of about 200 yards. After a detention of three-quarters of an hour, we again pushed on, and at a quarter-past 5, encamped in a small sandy bay on west, surrounded by detached rocks for 50 or 60 paces back, behind which, on either side the river, rose mountains almost perpendicular, and of incredible height, well clothed on the lower part with pine, fir, and cedar trees. Our course to-day is about south. The river made no great bends, but owing to occasional delays, and being often in strong eddies and whirlpools, our distance cannot be estimated at more than 50 miles. *At least half the distance the river is imbedded in the solid rock, and the other half is of bold rapids, with, however, plenty of water all over. The mountains, in no part of this day's work, recede from the very edge of the water, nor in no part was it more than a hundred and twenty paces in width, and often not quite half that.* The Indians descend by ladders to the river to fish"		
Above Simpson's Falls (5 or 6 miles)..	Oct. 10—Daylight		50	
Simpson's Falls..........	,, 10— ,, ...	Started at broad daylight, and in 25 minutes came to head of *Simpson's Falls, where the river is choked up by a most solid rock* of about half an acre in extent. Examined it along the west shore, but conceived the run on that side extremely dangerous, and, owing to the immense rocks all over, to carry was impossible. *The east lead was then determined upon; crossed; and run without landing, on that side, by the guide, who rushed on with his bark canoe, and a safe arrival below was effected, but not without much risk in the whirlpools against the rocks that hung over us.* The	5	

Sugar Loaf Mountain (probably at or near end of Canon)......	Oct. 10— 8 a.m......	boat followed, but did not suffer by the eddies so much as it did by being swallowed into the swell of the fall, out of which the utmost power of twelve paddles could not keep it. The second canoe also safely followed. A few hundred yards below this we came to the next and *last run*, which was steep, but uniform. Then the river began evidently to assume a different form. The water was settled, the beach flatter, and vegetation more profuse. At 8, passed a lofty rocky mountain, which, from its shape, we called Sugar Loaf Mountain. Say	15	3,106
		Continued descent till half-past 9, and landed for breakfast, which did not detain us 40 minutes. None of the small rivers to the left attracted our particular notice. At a quarter-past 2, passed the mouth of Lilliwhoet River, a stream of some size. Another river, half a league below, on opposite shore, which comes from the neighbourhood of Mount Baker. At half-past 3 o'clock *met the tide from Pacific Ocean*.	40	3,146
		Work's River on right at 5. Head of McMillan's Island at 7. FORT LANGLEY precisely at 8. Say	35	3,181
		[Note by Editor: Probably about 25 miles from the sea coast.]		
		Total canoe course	......	3,181
		Portages, including the one of 83 miles from McLeod's Fort to Fort St. James. Say	......	150

ITINERARY OF ROUTE (LAND AND WATER), *via* THOMPSON'S RIVER.

Fort Alexander	Sept. 27— 4·30 p.m.... ,, 28......	Started (with horses). Camped on second little stream...... Here the Governor (unwell) embarked with Mr. Yale to accompany him in the canoes three or four leagues further down. Encamped at 4, on Current River. Breakfasted at 20 miles from house.	4	2,782
34th Mile	,, 29— 6 a.m......	Started at 6. Passed two little rivers. Breakfasted on Main Stream (Note by Editor: Tributary) at 11. Resumed at 1; crossed and re-crossed in an hour after. Another little river at 2. A lake, half a mile, at 3. Encamped at within half a league of Long Lake. Road very good. Say	30	
64th Mile	,, 30— 5 a.m......	Started. Reached end of lake at 8. Left Main River at 9; breakfasted at Lake. Point of Woods took an hour. Arrived at large stream flowing to left. Crossed at a beaver dam, and continued on north bank for three hours to a lake, of which we made one mile, and camped. Say	30	

ITINERARY.—CANOE COURSE.—*Continued.*

Place.	Date. A.D. 1828.	Remarks.	Distance. Statute Miles.	Aggregates.
94th Mile.........	Oct. 1— 5.30 a.m.....	Lake took us to 8. Breakfasted at 9, on Main River. [Note by Editor: River flowing into North River.] Came to another lake at 2. Encamped at the other end at 4. In woods whole afternoon. Say.....	28	
122nd Mile.........	,, 2— 5.30 a.m.....	First half of road good, along a chain of lakes, but the last part was hilly and rocky. Small lake half a mile long. Lakes to-day seem still water. Afternoon, route a gradual ascent. Encamped at height.....	25	
147th Mile.........	,, 3— 6 a.m.........	Began to descend about 8; continued for a whole hour, coming down to the first small stream at foot, and in an hour more got to the *Traverse*.....	13	
"Traverse" (Ferry) of "North River" (North Branch of the Thompson.) Say 160 miles.....	....	Encamped. Say...... The Governor took canoe at the Traverse. We accompanied the horse brigade.	15	
175th Mile.........	Oct. 4.........	Horses could not be collected early. Governor and three men in canoe. Barrier Village by 8. Stockades about 11. Road not bad, and to the house is uncommonly fine. At the Pines all took horse. Arrived at house. [Editor's Note: "Fort Kamloops."].	40	
215th Mile.........	Oct. 6— 4 p.m.........	Started in boat, 12 paddles. Encamped at entrance of lake. Say.	7	
West end of Lake.........	,, 7— 4 a.m.........	Started. Reached other end of lake at a quarter to 8. Say. A number of minor rapids till we got to Bonaparte, 1 p.m. Remained an hour and a half with Indians. A little below, passed a dangerous rapid; three dalles by ¼ to 2. In half an hour, Observation or Wood Point, and Rapide Croche and Long Rapid by ¼ to 4. Coutamine Forks in another half hour. McDonald's Encampment at ¼ to 5. At 5, to shore for camp.....	13	2,997
Two miles below McDonald's Encampment.....	,, 8— 6 a.m.........	Started.	70	3,087
"Grand Forks" (of Fraser and Thompson).....	,, 8— 9 a.m.........	Arrived.	30	3,117
[For interval, see foregoing entries.] Fort Langley.........	,, 10— 8 p.m.........		144	3,261 3,261
		Total distance travelled by Governor Simpson and party......		

RECAPITULATION.

York Factory to Norway House	....	430 miles.
„ Head of Methy Portage	....	1,297 „
„ Fort Chipewyan	....	1,538 „
„ Dunvegan	....	2,108 „
„ Pass of Peace River, across line of Rocky Mountains	....	2,343 „
„ Fort St. James	....	2,578 „
„ „ Alexander	....	2,782 „
„ „ Kamloops	....	2,997 „
„ „ Forks Fraser and Thompson Rivers	....	3,117 „
„ „ Langley	....	3,261 „

CANOE COURSE.

Total, as per Itinerary	....	3,181 miles.

TIME.

Three months, less two days. Say	....	90 days.
Detention at posts	....	16 „
Total time *en route*	....	74 „
Detention of canoes at Forks of Fraser and Thompson River, waiting for land party	....	9 „
Total travelling time of canoes	....	65 „
Average per day, nearly	....	50 miles.

ITINERARY.—CANOE COURSE.—Continued.

Place.	Remarks.	Distance. Miles.	Average of river fall per mile.	Height. Feet above sea.
	ESTIMATES OF HEIGHTS.			
York Factory to Norway House.....	See Notes X., XI., XII. in Appendix. "Painted Rock"—*Roche Peinturée*			635
Lake Winnipeg........	See, besides the above Notes, Note XXXIX. in Appendix			630
Methy Portage (head)........	See Note XXXIV., and also XXX. in Appendix......			1,530
Athabasca Lake	See Note XXXIX. in Appendix......			600
Dunvegan ...	See Note LIII. in Appendix ...... This height is determined by Captain Lefroy; while Sir John Richardson puts it at only 770 feet. Thompson puts it at 1,000 feet where the thermometer he used for daily observation was, viz., in the Fort, on the top of the high bank.			910
	Deduct 20 miles from distance given in Itinerary from Chipewyan upwards, the nearest "mouth" of the Peace River being about that distance from it, and we have, as the distance from the mouth of the river to Dunvegan, as per Itinerary	550		
River at Rocky Mountain House	See Note LV. in Appendix; also Note LVIII., about middle. Distance above Dunvegan .... Height above Dunvegan, 420 feet. [This, I believe, is really a foot too much per mile.]	140	3 feet.	1,330
Head of Portage and Bend	See Note LVII. in Appendix. From river at Rocky Mountain House to head of Bend, by river, maximum ....; in fact, beyond reason, it may be said: $35 \times 6 = 210 + 1,330$. Rate of fall is also a "maximum,"	35	6 feet.	1,540
Pass of Peace River, through the Rocky Mountains......	From head of Portage .... Rate of fall, a liberal allowance...... $70 \times 3 = 210 + 1,540 = $ ...... HEIGHT OF PEACE RIVER PASS, 1,750 feet above the sea. See Note LVIII. in Appendix.	70	3 feet.	1,750
McLeod's Fort.........	Distance from Pass...... River course gentle and lacustrine......	152	1 foot.	

Fort St. James..................	152+1,750 = ...	......	......	1,902
	From McLeod's Fort...... : .... (say 102)−(omitting fractions),	83	1 ft. 3 in.	
	Estimated descent: 83×1¼ feet=103 (say 102)−(omitting fractions),			1,800
	1,902−102 = ...	......	......	
	This height is checked by calculations on the Fraser River course.			
	See Notes LXIV. and LXV. in Appendix.			
Fort Alexander..................	Thus: From Fort St. James, as per Itinerary	214		1,479
	Allow, as fair	......	1 ft. 6 in.	
	214×1½=321...1,800−321−			
Forks of Fraser and Thompson Rivers	From Fort Alexander (say 1½ feet in upper part to head of rapids, and	250	3 feet.	729
	the rest 4 feet average	......		
	250×3=750...1,479−750 =			
Sugar Loaf Mountain..............	From said Forks (canon and heading)......	74	9 feet.	63
	74×9=666...729−666 =	......		
Pacific "Tide"..................	From Sugar Loaf Mountain—allow 18 inches and a fraction per mile..	40	1·55 feet.	0
	40×1·55 feet=63 feet..63 ·63 =	......	......	

JOURNAL

OF

Canoe Voyage from Hudson's Bay to the Pacific.

BY THE LATE

SIR GEORGE SIMPSON,

Governor of the Honorable Hudson's Bay Company.

JOURNAL OF THE LATE ARCHIBALD MCDONALD, ESQUIRE, CHIEF FACTOR,
HONORABLE HUDSON'S BAY COMPANY, WHO ACCOMPANIED HIM.

YORK FACTORY, (*a*)
HUDSON'S BAY, A.D. 1828.

Saturday, 12th July.—At one a.m. the crews of two "Light Canoes,"(*b*)
consisting of nine men each, were in motion, carrying the provisions and
baggage to the water side ; and in a few minutes after, the Governor in
Chief,(*c*) Doctor Hamlyn and myself, were accompanied down to our craft
by fourteen commissioned gentlemen(*d*) and about as many clerks. After
something more than the usually cordial shake of the hand from all present, we embarked with three cheers under a salute of seven guns from
the Garrison, and against a strong tide, were soon round the first point
by the free use of the paddle and one of its accompanying "*voyageur*"
airs.

Our baggage and stores consist of

2 "Cassettes." (*e*)	2 Kegs Spirits.(*e*)
1 Paper Trunk.	2 ,, Porter.
1 Case.(*e*)	1 Tinnet Beef.
2 Baskets.(*e*)	1 Bag, fine pemican.
1 Bag, Bread.	2 Bags, pemican for men.
1 Bag, Biscuit.	2 Tents.

our three beds,(*e*) the mess cooking utensils, the usual "*agrès*"(*e*) for the
canoes, besides the men's own "*pactons.*"(*e*)

(*a*) See Appendix I.   (*b*) See Appendix II.   (*c*) See Appendix III.
(*d*) See Appendix IV.   (*e*) See Appendix V.

Breakfasted on Twenty Mile Island at eight. Took luncheon two points above Pennycataway River at one o'clock. Weather clear and warm. A few mosquitoes in evening. Encamped at the mouth of Steel River precisely at eight. The arrangement of the march has been handed over to us by the Governor. Doctor and myself, each night in turn, watch time, that we may start exactly at two in the morning.(*a*)   Men to have drams four times a day. Governor wrote a note to Mr. McTavish by two Indians drifting with fresh sturgeon for the use of the Fort, from whom we got one.   In the afternoon met two Athabasca loaded canoes.

Sunday, 13th.—Within a few minutes of two, the call was given, and precisely at the hour, were under weigh. With very little exception the men, the whole of the day and yesterday, "on the Line."(*b*)   The beach is fine and dry, but water remarkably low. Breakfast at eight, dinner at one, which last stoppage merely occupies from eight to ten minutes, that the men may swallow a mouthful of pemican, while the servant cuts off a slice of cold something with a glass of wine, to which the Governor invites one of his fellow travellers to partake of, as we move along and spend the remainder of the day on board his own canoe ; the other makes a very good shift to eat and drink something of the kind alone.   About this time to-day we got Colin Fraser to give us a few of his favorite strathspeys on the bagpipes, that went off very well to the ear of a High-lander, bnt as yet makes but a poor accordance with either the pole or the paddle.   This decent young man is lately from the Highlands, and on this voyage, accompanies the Governor in the double capacity of piper and assistant servant, &c.   In the afternoon, met the boats from English River, put ashore at eight, in a very good encampment, near the Sugar Loaf Bank.   Country hereabouts all on fire.

Monday, 14th.—Under weigh exactly at two.   Breakfast at Half-way Creek.   Arrived at Rock(*c*) at half-past three in the afternoon.   Had a peep at the Rock, an old establishment with its gardens.   Encamped late at the upper end of still water.   Met three Athabasca boats about noon.

Tuesday, 15th.—Shortly after leaving camp this morning, we passed a number of Indian families, living here the best way they can, till their husbands return from a trip to Norway House with goods.

In course of the day, while going up Hill River, spoke *L'Espérance* with two boats, Joe Bird with two, and Joe Cook two, all for Red River. (*d*)   From the foreman took two kegs of spirits for the use of our

---

party. Entered Swampy Lake at four, and encamped at Second Carrying place. Reached Jack River at the usual hour for camping. [Note by Ed. This is not the "Jack," *i.e.* Pike River, mentioned further on, but one called "Jack Tent River" by Thompson, and flows eastward, while the other, near whose mouth is Norway House, comes from the S.E. and strikes Winnipeg waters.]

Wednesday, 16th.—Commenced the passage of Knee Lake this morning at half-past three. Were abreast of the old depot at six. The small canoe dropping greatly behind, after rounding the Knee, the crews exchanged canoes by way of trial. The Governor's men with much ado, pushed the small canoe ahead. A gust of wind, accompanied with rain and lightening, put us ashore, where we remained for two hours. Arrived at Trout Fall by eight, and met the "White Governor [a *soubriquet* of the man at the head of the boat brigade] and a party here. They took twenty-seven days to Jack River (Norway House), and this is their ninth day downwards. Their cargo is robes (buffalo), and a few packs of "rats." Governor Simpson bespoke two Indians to go down to meet L'Espérance, and replace two disabled men in his boats.

Thursday, 17th.—Got off half-an-hour later than usual, in consequence of the shoal water and numerous bad stones in this river. The Governor's canoe touched some time after starting, whereupon we had to put ashore and gum canoe ; about an hour after, our canoe struck, and it was with great difficulty we gained the shore dry. The Governor pushed on, and we remained for the space of two and a half hours, sewing in two large pieces. Came up with the other canoe opposite Nine Mile Island at half-past ten. Each of us *en passant* took a little flour at Oxford House for the men, and exchanged the York Factory pemican, which was very bad indeed, for better. Got to Wippimpanish at half-past five. Head wind on the Lake. Encamped late near Windy Lake.

The experiment of yesterday having proved that the Governor's canoe was not only better manned, but also a better going craft, he exchanged two good hands for two inferior ones, and throughout the whole of this day's journey, the two canoes seem to go much alike.

Friday, 18th.—Did not start before half-past two. Got to Hill Portage at half-past five, left at six, and reached the White Fall a quarter before ten, when we made rather a late breakfast. Dried our tents, &c., here. Left the upper end a little before noon, and arrived at the Painted Stone (*a*) by three o'clock. The water was low at Aitchemanus.(*b*) Encamped

---

(*a*) See Appendix X.   (*b*) See Appendix XI.

late below the upper beaver dam. This has been a very warm day, and we found no mosquitoes in this acknowledged nursery for them. The Governor shot a few ducks during the day.

Saturday, 19th.—We had thunder, with heavy showers of rain, last night and this morning, which is the first weather of the kind since we commenced the journey. The water being secured at one of the dams, we carried canoes and all. Breakfast at nine o'clock at the mouth of Black Water Creek. Sailed up Sea River.(*a*) Changed, [*i.e.* changed dress for arrival at port,] and dined above the portage. As we waft along under easy sail, the men with a clean change and mounting new feathers, the Highland bagpipes in the Governor's canoe, was echoed by the bugle in mine ; then these were laid aside, on nearer approach to port, to give free scope to the vocal organs of about eighteen Canadians (French) to chant one of those voyageur airs peculiar to them, and always so perfectly rendered. Our entry to Jack River House(*b*) (Norway House) about seven p.m., was certainly more imposing than anything hitherto seen in this part of the Indian country. Immediately on landing, His Excellency was preceded by the piper from the water to the Fort, while we were received with all welcome by Messrs. Chief Trader McLeod and Dease, (*c*) Mr. Robert Clouston, and a whole host of ladies.

We here got some little things arranged for the voyage. The Governor was occupied in writing the whole of the evening.

NORWAY HOUSE.

Sunday 20th.—Blowing fresh last night and this morning, with occasional showers of rain. Did not start before eleven a.m. Took in the following stores here, viz. :—$23\frac{1}{2}$ lbs. cheese, 13 lbs. hyson tea, 1 lb. mustard, 84 lbs. ham, 4 one gallon kegs port wine, 3 one gallon kegs of madeira, 21 lbs. butter, 2 casks biscuit, (fine and common) each 56 lbs., 1 keg port wine, 1 keg spirits for the men, and left the two borrowed from L'Espérance's boats on the 15th. The canoes, between them, had two bags pemican, two bags flour, and a keg of pork from the Governor's stores, besides a few little necessaries for the use of the canoes. Strong head wind in the Play Green Lake(*d*). Arrived at Warren's Point at four p.m., but cannot commence the " Big Lake." [Winnipeg].

Monday, 21st.—Weather moderate. Got under weigh about four a.m.

(*a*) See Appendix XII.   (*b*) See Appendix XIII.
(*c*) See Appendix XIV,   (*d*) See Appendix XV,

There was a little wind, rather ahead all day ; still we got the length of the first Limestone Point.

Tuesday, 22nd.—Wind continued ahead. Got to mouth of river [Saskatchewan] for breakfast by nine. Got everything to the upper end of the Grand Rapid (*a*) by about three p.m., where we remained about an hour, drying everything we had, which had undergone a complete soaking for the space of two hours' incessant rain, while ascending the rapid. Traded a few pieces fresh sturgeon from the *Freeman* (*b*) for a little tobacco, besides a note to one of them, Thomas, for pork. Mounted the Upper Rapids. Got over Cross Lake, and encamped at the head of Cross Lake Rapid.

Wednesday, 23rd.—Made a start about the usual time. Weather fine. Passed the *Détroit* by five. Breakfasted on a long Point of Cedars in Bourbon Lake at eight. Commenced the *traverse* (*c*) without loss of time, and were fortunate enough to gain the shore in the next narrows before a thunderstorm with rain came on which obliged us to put ashore, unload, and go under cover (*d*) for an hour and a half. Clearing up towards three o'clock, we resumed the journey ; crossed the lower Muddy Lake, and encamped on *L'Isle de Festins.* Doctor Hamlyn, who complained a little yesterday evening, had been very unwell the whole of this day, proceeding from a bowel complaint. Left our frying pan in last night's encampment.

Thursday, 24th.—A couple of hours after leaving the encampment, we discovered ourselves out of the proper channel, and with the view of gaining it, penetrated more than a mile across, through reeds and long grass, (*e*) until we reached the Upper Muddy Lake, over which we had to drag the canoes a considerable distance before we got into the regular lead of the water. My canoe was a little crushed, over a stump in this lake, and had to be gummed, at the breakfast hour on *L'Ile d'Epinette.* Encamped early at the upper end of *L'Ile d'Epinette,* where we had some difficulty to unload.

Friday, 25th.—The last, is the only dry night (*f*) we have had since leaving Norway House, yet it does not appear to presage settled weather. The whole of this forenoon has been nothing but showers and peals of thunder. Stopped on shore at the *Passe* for a moment when we got a few " gold eyes," [a kind of fresh herring about a foot long, with bright iris, large and yellow—Indian name, Nacaish,] and some pieces of dried

---

(*a*) See Appendix XVI.   (*b*) See Appendix XVII.   (*c*) See Appendix XVIII.
(*d*) See Appendix XIX,   (*e*) See Appendix XX.   (*f*) See Appendix XXI.

meat from Constant, for which we gave him a note on Mr. Leith, to
settle with him.   At dinner time one of the Governor's men submitted
to the operation of having a tooth drawn by Dr. Hamlyn, which was
soon done.   Put up about two leagues below the *Barrière,* on a small
patch of dry ground, which is rather a rare comfort in this part of the
country.   Shot three or four pigeons and as many ducks.

Saturday, 26th.—Got under weigh by two o'clock.   Came about six or
seven leagues and breakfasted, which is about the same distance to Cumberland House.   Blowing fresh on the Lake, and shipped water before we
gained the shore, which we did at half-past two.   Remained here, drying
baggage, for the rest of the day.

Sunday, 27th.—Here [Cumberland House] (*a*) took in, for the trip,
each canoe a bag of common pemican, and for the mess, a bag of dried
meat (50 lbs.,) and 80 buffalo tongues, besides old and new potatoes,
eggs, candles, and 4 gallons of spirits for the men.   Got under weigh at
half-past three, with fair weather, and a touch up of a favorite song
chorused by both canoes.   Breakfasted on one of the islands.   Here the
guide (*b*) expressed a desire to have a better division of the men in favor
of his own canoe, upon which, the Governor, in fairness to both, directed
that they should be called out one by one by the two former, which was
done, but ultimately placed both canoes nearly as they stood before the
change made on the 17th.   Entered *Riviere Maligne* about noon.   On
Rat Portage passed two Indian lodges from Rat country ; offered us a
little dried meat which we declined, but gave them a dram and a little
tobacco.   Encamped on Sturgeon Rock below Beaver Lake.   Water
tolerably good in this river.

Monday, 28th.—Did not start before three.   Entered Beaver Lake at five.
Fine clear weather.   Breakfasted on one of the islands.   Commenced
Portage de Pins at half-past ten.   Reached Carp Portage at five o'clock ;
made the Birch Portage and several strong rapids before we got to
another stretch of still water, where we put up a little before eight.   Had
much thunder, and, now and then, tremendous heavy showers of rain.
Saw a few Indians along the banks of the river, to whom we spoke *en
passant.*

Tuesday, 29th.—Made an early start, being in good water, and before
six got over the Island and Pine Portages, Lake Heron, which took us
two hours.   Breakfasted in the *Détroit* at eight.   In two hours more we

---

(*a*) See Appendix XXII.   (*b*) See Appendix XXIII.

crossed Pelican Lake. From eleven to twelve made the three short portages, and after making *Portage des Bois* in a very heavy shower of rain, we dined while gumming at the upper end. The Lake of this name took us seven hours. Encamped late, near bye Portage.

Wednesday, 30th.—Being close to the first portage, we did not start before daylight. Breakfasted at the head of the first grand rapid in English River (*a*) or Churchill waters, into which we fell after making the portage this morning. Lost one of our paddles in the *Barril* Portage, half way between *Portage des Iles* and the Rapid River carrying places. Dined at one. Saw a number of black bears here, but they made for the woods. Picked a good many ripe raspberries, currants and gooseberries on the portages to-day. Showers of rain all day. Arrived at Rapid River by four o'clock, where we remained nearly an hour for Mr. Heron, who embarked with us for Athabasca. Here we took 45 lbs. fine pemican, and a few pieces of dried meat. Got up little *Discharge* in good time, and encamped at about three leagues from the Rapid River House.

Thursday, 31st.—Got under weigh at three o'clock. Made the Mountain Portage early, and before breakfast passed the Pine and other Rapids. In the forenoon, made the "Devil's Portage," at the head of which, my canoe had to be gummed, which caused a detention of half an hour. After dinner we made a number of hauling places before coming to Trout Portage, in one of which the Governor's canoe took a sheer, and was nearly being dashed against the rock. At half-past seven o'clock encamped upon a green hill about half way across the Lake. [Probably on one side of the lake.] The piper gave us a few marches before supper. This is admitted to have been a hard day's work. Thermometer in shade at noon, 70°. Mr. Heron took his turn to watch last night.

Tuesday, 1st August.—Started at half past two o'clock, and got to Portage de H——, [possibly *Portage de Halliers*, Thicket Portage.] *Lac Mille d'Ours* took us to three p.m., and made *Portage Femme.* Pine Lake took us an hour ; crossed that portage also. Head wind in *Lac de Souris.* Put up on the sandy point, a fine dry encampment, where we picked up a good many berries.

Saturday, 2nd.—Made an early move to-day. Got over Serpent Rapid, Sandy Lake, Grassy River, Rapide Milieu and Rapid Croche. A hard day's work. Governor shot a pelican, (*b*) a few ducks, and a couple of geese. Our second keg of spirits from York Factory was done.

(*a*) See Appendix **XXIV**.   (*b*) See Appendix **XXV**.

Sunday, 3rd.—Got under weigh about the usual hour.   Crossed Lake Primeau, breakfasted at the head of Portage des Pins. Here the men were found to be entirely out of provisions, having of their own accord [*Sic* in M.S. but of course it must have been inadvertently, that the men—of a class, characteristically and necessarily careful in such matters of life and death in those wilds, so dropt their "prog" on the way] left at Rapid River half of the pemican provided to each canoe.   After a sharp lecture upon their imprudent conduct, and an assurance from them never to be guilty of so much indifference to their own absolute wants again, some dried meat of our own was served out for the day.   At half-past one, got to head of *Portage de Souris*, [or *Source*, it is impossible to make out some of the names in French in the M.S.]   Got over the Shaggunnu by five o'clock ; day excessively warm. Encamped at Point de Gervais near the Straits.

Monday, 4th.—Breakfasted and changed at Point au Sable. Arrived at Fort (*a*) of *Isle à la Crosse* by eleven a.m. where we found Mr. Deschambeault and the family of Mr. Chief Factor Charles. Remained for the day arranging our canoes, &c. Cadotte not yet returned from Portage La Loche, though it is now seventeen days since he passed on : last year he was here on his way back by the first.

The Governor writing letters for the lower country. Here we take in the following provisions, viz.:

2 Casks fine Biscuits, each 56 lbs.	10 lbs. Shot.
1 Keg Madeira Wine.	1 lb. Gun Powder.
10 lbs. Hyson Tea.	4 lbs. Ball.
3 Bags com. pemican, each 85 lbs	$\frac{1}{2}$ doz. Gun Worms.
70 lbs. fine „	12 Flints.
165 lbs. Dried Meat.	2 lbs. Twist Tobacco.
40 lbs. Flour, common, for men.	20 lbs. Gum.
3 Skins Lodge Leather.	40 pairs Shoes.
A large bark Canoe, to be returned.	

Will also form a third Canoe here on account of the low water in River *La Loche.*

Tuesday, 5th.—Got under weigh at half-past three a.m. with unusual glee in the three canoes. Just as we were putting ashore for breakfast, Cadotte cast up with his three boats from the Portage with 157 packs(*b*) and 3 kegs Castorum, the returns of the McKenzie's River District for outfit 1827.

(*a*) See Appendix XXVI.   (*b*) See Appendix XXVII.

After being two days there, Mr. Chief Factor Smith (Edward) arrived on the 26th ultimo, remained with him (Cadotte) five days, getting the packs across, and left on the evening of the 31st. He believes Mr. Smith would have been able to leave the other end of the Portage yesterday. Dined at the narrows of *Lac du Bœuf* at three. Head wind all day. Encamped at a point N.W. of the old Fort, it being too late to attempt a large traverse to the east shore, and there being every appearance of bad weather.

Wednesday, 6th.—It was not yet two o'clock this morning when we made a move against a strong head wind, which towards day-light increased to a gale, with heavy rain, and which rendered our landing on one of the points within a few leagues of the river *La Loche*, a matter of some difficulty. Breakfasted early, and waited for a moderation in the weather till about ten, when we again took to our canoes and gained the river by noon. Were at the Forks of Pembina River at half-past three. Commenced McLeod's Portage near five o'clock, and reached the upper end all safe before eight. Fine weather in the afternoon. Killed a few rabbits along the banks of the river. Water remarkably low.

Thursday, 7th.—Cold frosty(*a*) morning. Water still the same until we got to the Lake about two p.m. where we left the *Isle à la Crosse* canoe, and a note for Mr. Stuart. (*b*) Sailed across the Lake, about half-way met fifteen or twenty Chipweyan Indians with their wives and families in as many canoes. Ten of them joined us in the evening at the second *Pose* [resting place in a long portage, from the French word reposer to rest] close to the little creek, and will give us a lift on this portage of twelve miles(*c*) to-morrow. They say that Mr. Smith left the other end three days ago.

Friday, 8th,—About four o'clock a.m. made a start. The eight "bouts' (i.e. men of the ends including steersmen and bowsmen, called " boots" from the French word *bout*, end) carrying the canoes, and the other five men of each of the canoes (only two canoes seem to have been carried over) with the assistance of the ten Indians in carrying the loading, were able to remove everything in one haul (trip, " *voyage* " is the usual term) by a succession of " *poses* " of 500 to 600 yards each.(*d*) We reached the south shore of Little Lake by nine, where we breakfasted. This Lake is about two miles in circumference, and is two thirds of the distance. We crossed it with canoes and baggage about eleven, and the last one-third

---

(*a*) See Appendix XXVIII.   (*b*) See Appendix XXIX.
(*c*) See Appendix XXX.   (*d*) See Appendix XXXI.

took us till two p.m. but the canoes and Indians did not arrive before
four. We gummed for three quarters of an hour, and again embarked.
Made the whole of the Mud Portage by seven, and encamped, that the
men may enjoy two or three extra glasses of spirits to-night, which they
would have had in making the portage had we had no Indians about us.
Before parting with the latter, we settled with them in the most satisfac-
tory manner (to them). First, the Governor addressed them at some
length on their good behaviour since they have become reduced to one
tráding house,(a) the good policy of continuing so, the propriety of discontinuing the use of spirituous liquors,(b) and ended in pointing out to
them the expediency of nursing the beaver in their lands. After giving
each, as a matter of great indulgence, a glass of weak rum, they got notes
on Mr. Chief Factor Charles at *Isie à la Crosse* for a fathom of tobacco,
&c. This has been a fine dry day, and not too warm. [No wonder—
It was a cold frosty morning the day before!] Delightful prospect (c)
down this river. [Clear Water River, one of the numerous sources of
the many branched great McKenzie River].

Saturday, 9th.—Did not start the men before four, in consequence of
the fatigues of yesterday. Were under weigh at a quarter to five. Got
over Portage *de Pins* and *La Bonne Rapide* before seven. Breakfasted
at the head of a cascade, where we carried a few pieces for three-quarters
of a mile. Dined in the usual way as we dropped down. Water low in
this place. Passed the mouth of Pembina River at half-past five. Encamped late, within a couple of leagues of the big Athabasca River.(d)
Killed a cat, [Note by Ed.—Lynx probably, for there are no cats, *eo nomine*,
in that quarter, but there is a rocky mountain cat, an animal with a fearful yell, called *Pichon* by the French Canadians, whose habitat is considered as confined to the Rocky Mountains, four hundred miles off, and to
their slope and plains where wooded, at the foot of the mountains. The
animal is about the size of an ordinary sized dog, fawn colored, and spot-
ted like a panther—hence also called panther cat. However, it is possible that the animal, of wandering habit like all felines, may have got
thus far in search of food.] This is the only quadruped(e) we have seen
since the bears in English River.

Sunday, 10th.—Head wind. Thunderstorm with flashes of lightning
and tremendous fall of rain throughout the night. The water being
shoal, we did not start before four o'clock. Arrived at the Grand River

---

(a) See Appendix XXXII.   (b) See Appendix XXXIII.   (c) See Appendix XXXIV.
(d) See Appendix XXXV.   (e) See Appendix XXXVI.

[*Grande Rivière*] Athabasca, which we found "good water." Fine runs along the river. Passed Red River and the Little Hills opposite at half-past ten o'clock. Passed the Bituminous Springs (*a*) on right, about noon, and reached *Pierre au Calumet* (pipe stone), on left hand at two o'clock. Had the pleasure of passing this afternoon on board with the Governor. About four o'clock a heavy dark cloud in the south-west indicated the approach of a storm which, in a few minutes, poured down upon us in hail stones of at least the size of a small pistol ball, and continued for about twenty-five minutes. The evening wet, cold, and chilly. Encamped on Poplar Point. *Large strata of Pit Coal* (*b*) *all along either side of* the River. Not an Indian on this communication, and strange to say, not even the appearance of an animal.

Monday, 11th.—Started after three. Breakfasted at eight, about nine miles above *L' Embarras*, which we passed at half-past ten, leaving the old fort of Mr. Ross nearly opposite on the right hand. At one o'clock, White Fish Creek on the right. Did not enter Athabasca Lake (*c*) before five. Crossed with the poles. Strong head wind. Changed [*i.e.* dressed for arrival in proper trim] on Coal Island, and arrived at Fort Chippawian (*d*) [Chipewyan] by seven, where we found Mr. William McGillivray. Mr. Smith arrived here from the portage with his three boats two days ago. The Indians were much pleased to see their old trader, Mr. Simpson, once more among them. It is just a month since we left York Factory.(*e*)　New, but very small potatoes.

Tuesday, 12th.—Boisterous weather during the whole of last night and to-day. Men could do nothing to their canoes. Mine remains here, and we take another in its stead of rather a larger size. Mr. Smith leaves this in a couple of days for McKenzie's River. The present system of transport between that part of the interior and York Factory is an admirable one. Mr. Smith went down from the Forks or Fort Simpson to Fort Good Hope, with two boats for the returns in the latter end of May. Left it on his way back on the fourth of June. *En passant* took in the packs of Mr. Brisebois at Fort Norman. Got back to Fort Simpson on the 17th, where he took in the furs of the place and those of Mr. McPherson procured up the south branch at *Fort de Liards*, and made a final start on the 19th, with the whole returns of that district in three boats—say 160 packs exclusive of twenty-five that remain inland for want of means to carry them out. Mr. Smith arrived at Slave Lake

<hr>

(*a*) See Appendix XXXVII. (*b*) See Appendix XXXVIII. (*c*) See Appendix XXXIX. (*d*) See Appendix XL. (*e*) See Appendix XLI.

[Great Slave Lake] on the 3rd of July, and at Fort Chipwayan [so in M. S.]—reached Portage La Loche on the 26th, where Cadotte with three boats and the outfit from York Factory, had been, two days previous. He was eight days on the portage, and of course, returned from this end on the 4th of August.

Wednesday, 13th.—Weather much changed. Making every preparation to start to-morrow. The Governor closed his public correspondence for the season this side of the Rocky Mountains, (*a*) among which is a Chief Factor's Commission to Mr. Peter Warren Dease (*b*). All the Chipwayans are within reach of the Fort, and came in to-day and had an audience with the Governor. Mr. James Heron was introduced to them as the successor of Mr. William McGillivray, who accompanies us to-morrow for the west side of the mountains, family and all. All the buildings about this place are in a state of decay. Gardens not very extensive.

Note of sundries received at Fort Chipwyan :—

4 Bags Pemican,	40 lbs. Gum,
10 lbs. Grease, 21 lbs. Dried Meat,	20 lbs. Grease for ditto,
7 quarts Salt,	2 Large Axes in use,
5 lbs. Tobacco,	1 Flat File, (12 inches)
5 lbs. Beaver Shot.	5 Rusty Clasp Knives,
1½ lbs. Gunpowder,	12 Dressed Skins, [to make]
1½ lbs. Gun Flints,	74 Pairs Indian Shoes.

All on account of general expenses, Northern Department.

The following are charged to the Columbia Department for supplies to men as per account :—12 lbs tobacco, &c.

Thursday, 14th.—Constant rain again the whole of this forenoon, and could not start before half-past twelve. Mr. McGillivray embarks with the Doctor, and I have the honor of taking a place with the Governor in his canoe. Our departure from Fort Chipwyan—the grand emporium of the North in days of yore—was as imposing as the firing of guns, heavy cheers from master and men on the rocks, and the waving of flags, and songs in abundance on our part could make it. Left at two, on our right, English Island, where Mr. Peter Fidler formerly built, and whose chimnies still stand. At three o'clock entered the small river whose current at present is with us. Dined. The evening threatening a violent storm, to make the best of it, we encamped early at the end of the portage that leads to the House [Fort] in winter.

(*a*) See Appendix XLII.   (*b*) See Appendix XLIII.

Friday, 15th.—Watch was again regularly kept. Got under weigh at three. Fell into Peace River in an hour after, and which of course, we now ascend. Breakfasted a little below Point Providence. [The names of places in the manuscript are sometimes difficult to make out ; this is one.] Beach muddy and dirty, and of which, I understand, we shall have abundance before we reach Dunvegan. I believe that it was from this point that most of the party sent down from the falls [Mountain Fall] by Mr. Clarke [late chief Factor, John Clarke, of Montreal,] perished in 1815, on their way down to Fort Wedderburn. Weather pretty fine to-day. A solitary swan, the only game in the course of this day's march, passed us. It received eight or ten shots from us, but to no purpose. Encamped on *Isle de Plâtre*. [So called, probably, from the plastery nature of the soil.]

Saturday, 16th.—Made a move at two. Breakfasted on a small island where Mr. John George McTavish was taken by the ice in the fall of 1818. Jack Fish Creek on our right at noon. John's house nearly opposite. Saw two or three flocks of geese, but killed none. Two Cree families encamped on the island below *Grande Marie*. Gave us nothing.

Sunday, 17th.—Soon after starting, came to another camp of Crees of ten or twelve lodges ; they had nothing but a few scraps of very indifferent meat, which we paid for three-fold in tobacco. Breakfasted above Mr. McTavish's House. Light showers all day. Could distinctly see the Cariboo Mountains at a distance, to our right (*a*). Killed a couple of young geese. Early to-night, the Northern Lights have been seen to very great advantage. Often a complete arch from east to west, of the most brilliant columns sprang up, and as often dispersed (*b*).

Monday, 18th.—Breakfasted below Cariboo River, which we left on our right about noon. At three, passed Wolf Point. A few minutes before we arrived at the Falls, left Red River on our left. Made portage at six, and at the upper carrying place, arrived with canoes, baggage and all, not before eight, where we found the recent encampment of Beaver Indians. The Fall [called the Mountain Fall, and also Grand Falls] is a grand sheet of water, about half a mile across, and perhaps ten or fifteen feet high (*c*). Last of men's rum finished to-day.

Tuesday, 19th.—Breakfasted opposite Loon River, below the " Eng" [English ?] old house built by Halcro. Three hours after that, passed Colville House, then Mr. Clarke's Point, and after that, about four

---

(*a*) See Appendix XLIV.   (*b*) See Appendix XLV.   (*c*) See Appendix XLVI.

o'clock, Boyer's River, Upper Cariboo River, and Old Fort Liard, all in succession on our right. Encamped early on a fine high bank. In the course of the day the foreman of the second canoe was called to account for not keeping up with the other, which seems to have had the effect of spurring them on the remainder of the day. This, besides another, is the only fine day *throughout* we have had since leaving Norway House.

Wednesday, 20th.—Started early. Breakfasted above big *Pointe de Roche*, and dined near the little point of the same name, near old Fort de Tremble. At the C—— by six ; Long Island, which is half way to the House, about eight ; and did not arrive at Fort Vermilion (*a*) before ten, where we found Mr. Paul Fraser and two men, and here also we got a sumptuous supper of hot moose steaks and potatoes.

Thursday, 21st.—Remain here all day, which gives the men an opportunity of refreshing themselves. This is by far, the finest day but one, since we left Norway House. In addition to which, we have had the good chance to find the greatest part of a fresh moose here, which, with the acquisition of potatoes affords them (the men) a delicious meal. Sent the interpreter and a young half-breed up the river to the Fort hunters requesting that they may have an animal or two for us to-morrow evening. In the afternoon, three of the Beaver Indians came in and were amused at everything they saw about us, the doctor's percussion gun, and our various musical instruments. They seem to have good gardens here, in potatoes and barley.

Friday, 22nd.—Did not start before six a.m. Left the Keg Creek on our right by ten ; Iroquois and Goose Rivers at eleven and twelve. Dined below Wolverine Point, and soon after fell in with the canoes sent to the hunters yesterday, who informed us that up to that time nothing had been killed, but that in all probability we should find them with something towards evening, higher up. Accordingly, by seven o'clock, on point *Hangard à l'Eau* [shed or outhouse on the water,] we found the two with a moose, (*b*) which our men soon carried from the woods. Encamped. The hunters were well rewarded by notes on the Fort and a little tobacco from ourselves.

Saturday, 23rd.—Were under weigh early. Breakfasted at L'Isle de Landrie. Dined at L'Isle de Perche, and encamped two miles above Battle River. Constant showers since we left the Fort. Men feast well.

Sunday, 24th.—Breakfasted below old Fort feu à cheval, [Fort fire on horseback is unintelligible, but so it is written, and the editor has no

---

(*a*) See Appendix XLVII.   (*b*) See Appendix XLVIII.

means of finding what is meant ; none of the maps at his command shew it, and he has the very best, including that made by the celebrated Arrowsmith—prince of map makers—for the Hudson's Bay Company out of plans, maps, and reports, &c., furnished by the Company itself.] Here, in former days, Messrs. Clarke and Black had a recontre. Put ashore on a dirty gravelly beech below *Ile de Campement*, and at this moment (eleven p.m.) the torrent of rain, with wind and lightening, is tremendous.

Monday, 25th.—Stormy morning, did not start before four. Breakfasted at Cadotte's River. Encamped at the Spring Islands, near Mr. Colin Campbell's House, early, that ourselves and men may make things a little comfortable and strong after the ducking of last night and this morning. The River in this part seems imbedded in sand-stone rock, which shows on both sides ; the sand-stone here and there emitting large columns of black earth(*a*) in [on] the hills from above the margin of the rock. [The description is given in the *ipsissima verba* of the M.S. in case the phenomenon, one so strange, yet not unaccountable, should be misrepresented by an alteration of terms or construction of sentence.]

Tuesday, 26th.—Made a move about three. Breakfasted a little below the lost St. Mary's House, which is nearly opposite *Rivière le C——* We all walked along the beach for some distance, from Mr. Robertson's, St. Mary's, which we passed at eleven a.m., and which is directly facing Clarke's original St. Mary's at the mouth of Smoky River.(*b*) Dined at an old Fort of Mr. David Thompson's, and encamped at the Six Islands with a freeman called *Bastonais*, who gave us a little bear's meat and berries. This is a delightful country, that we have passed through to-day.(*c*) Passed through crops of berries, "*poires*" or sascutum berries (*d*) all along the bank of the river.

Wednesday, 27th.—Started early so as to arrive at the Fort to-night, in which object we were much assisted by the unusual fine weather, but the breaking of one of our canoes retarded us some time. Saw a couple of bears at a distance. Towards evening the appearance of half-a-dozen horses convinced us we were near *Dunvegan*, (*e*) which we accordingly reached at sunset, and took Mr. Campbell by surprise.

Thursday, 28th.—We remain here for the day, allowing the men to recruit : but unfortunate it is, that there is at this moment no fresh meat at the place, and that we can only make up for the deficiency, in

---

(*a*) See Appendix XLIX.   (*b*) See Appendix L.   (*c*) See Appendix LI.
(*d*) See Appendix LII.   (*e*) See Appendix LIII

good dried meat for them. But as animals are very numerous in the neighbourhood, the Indian hunters were dispatched this morning to make what havoc they can amongst them. The two men of the Fort, with the assistance of our own, made thirteen bags of pemican, enough with what we had on hand, to start with on our voyage, and we trust at the same time to the success of the hunters for a little more. We mean to start to-morrow.

This establishment was abandoned in the fall of 1824, in consequence of the death(a) of Mr. Guy Hughes and four men at St. Johns in the fall of 1823, and Fort Vermilion alone was kept in Peace River. A certain end by this measure being gained. Dunvegan was re-established by Mr. Campbell.

The Fort was found perfectly entire, and the Beaver Indians have ever since evinced the most friendly and submissive disposition. Indeed from the commencement of this unfortunate affair, the Indians of the two lower establishments could not strictly be charged with any share in the massacre at St. John's. Many are the opinions, and indeed many of them very opposite, relative to this melancholy subject. Whoever were the perpetrators, and however substantial the proof against any of them, such it is, that three or four of the St. John's Indians have kept aloof ever since; frequenting the country along the edge of mountains between the head waters of the River de Liard, and the mouth of Finlay's Branch.

Upon such an occasion as this, it could not be supposed that the Governor would pass through the country without adverting to those outrages, and recommending proper conduct in future on the part of all the Indians of this quarter. This was done in due form through La Fleur, the Interpreter, to as many of them (seven or eight) as were present this evening.

The frolics of old, from liquor, were in like manner alluded to, and in particular that which led to the death of an Indian at this place some years ago. They appeared much pleased with what is said to them. The sound of the bugle, the bagpipes, Highland Piper in full dress, the musical suuff box, &c., excited in them emotions of admiration and wonder. They got a little tobacco, and a very weak drop of rum and water with sugar.

Friday, 29th.—The hunters returned late last night with a moose, but being less than the quantity expected, we take an additional two bales of meat. Our whole supplies here are as follows, viz:

(a) See Appendix LIV.

50 Pairs Indian Shoes.

10 Bags common pemican.

  3 ,,   fine with berries.

  1 quart gunpowder and 100 balls.

  7 bales dried meat, each 85 lbs. including 1 to Gentlemen, of only 80 lbs.

39 lbs. Grease, exclusive of 4 lbs. for gum.

  7 Dressed Skins, including one for Cords.

72 lbs. Dried Meat, rations for Men.

  2 Parchment Skins, as wrappers.

  1 Canoe Awl.

  1 Moose Deer—fresh meat.

12 Skins per order of Governor

Had an early breakfast, and after taking leave of the new Chief Trader, (for Mr. Campbell was one of the batch of this season,) we took our departure in three canoes, the third canoe we bring the length of the portage, finding that we would be too much encumbered in the two canoes. Saw several bears in the course of the day, and we also fancied we saw the buffalo. Killed nothing. Raining most of the afternoon. Encamped early below the islands without name.

Saturday, 30th.—Made an early start. Strong current(*a*) all day. Weather very fine. Great appearance of Beaver. Saw several lodges in main river. Bears numerous along the hills, one crossed the river before us, but gained the shore before we could be at him. Breakfasted in front of a hill on main river, to which it is said, the Red Deer is peculiar in this quarter. Encamped at *La Grève* near the river.

Sunday, 31st.—Breakfasted on Pemican Island, and dined about 500 yards below Fort *d'Epinette :* near the same distance above it, the same side, is *Rivière d'Epinette* (Pine River) a stream of some size. Encamped within a short distance of Mr. Yale's House on the left hand. Did not land at St. John's were the people were murdered. Saw the houses and a cross(*b*) or two on the beach. About five o'clock spoke two Indians of the beaver tribe, with their families, from whom we obtained some berries and a little bear's meat : a third Indian belongs to the band, and according to the information of the others was out hunting to-day, but we apprehend that to be a " fitch," and that he made it a point to be off with himself as we landed, being in some degree involved in the mystery attending the murder. His name is Sancho. He was much enraged at Mr. Black for taking away one of his wives a few days prior to the sanguinary deed ; was present when the Indians fired at Messrs. Black and Henry's canoes going off from St. John's, and is, at all events, the brother

---

(*a*) See Appendix LV.   (*b*) See Appendix LVI.

of two Indians that have not been seen since, and are universally charged as the murderers. Those we saw, seemed good Indians. For the meat they gave us, they had notes on the Fort.

Monday, September 1st.—Started at half-past three. At five passed the *Grande Fourche* which we had on the left. Breakfasted below the Red Stone Rock, on the same side. Doctor and myself ashore to-day, and had much misery. River D———— on right. *Rivière la Petite Tête*, on same side at five. Camped at seven. Current strong. Fine dry day. Saw many beaver lodges in the morning. Through the night they [beaver] were working and plunging in the river. Our canoe from Dunvegan goes very indifferently.

Tuesday, 2nd.—Thick morning. Fired, but to no purpose, at four red deer this morning. Left another *Grande Fourche* on the right. Breakfasted one point above *Rivière Maligne*. Dined on *Ile de Pierre*. Soon after had a glance of the Rocky Mountains (*a*) a few leagues off. Current not so strong to-day. Arrived at the portage at five. [N. B.— First portage, save that only other one from the mouth of Peace River, viz. : that at the Grand Falls of " ten or fifteen feet" fall, already reported.] Immediately, eight men with the two canoes proceeded by water, and with the remaining ten we made the first *pose* of the portage with something like forty pieces. Encamped on the first fine level above the water, and have the old Mountain House right opposite on the south side. Near where we landed, the rocks in several places, poured out spouts of water as if coming from the mouth of a gun.

Wednesday, 3rd.—By four, the canoes were under weigh. Reached the top of the last high bank and breakfasted at eleven. About a mile of the worst road in Christendom. After midday, resumed the journey, and with unspeakable misery to the poor men got to a small swamp, a little more than another mile. Ourselves, however, with the necessary baggage, pushed on to a little clear stream ahead, not quite half a mile, and encamped late. No people having passed this way for the last three years, and, of course, no clearance made in a road that at best must be an infamous one, presented a horrible appearance to-day, and whatever be the fate of the canoes and men by water, I think, of the two evils, they have chosen the least ; in fact, without considerable labour, the way would be impracticable for passing the canoes. [*Id est*, for passing canoes *overland*.] A large moose buck passed us in the woods this morning.

(*a*) See Appendix LVII.

Thursday, 4th.—Returned early to men left behind last night, and got all on to Little Creek by eight, without further delay to them than in taking a good draught of water. Carried on very well, on tolerably clear ground, till we came to another watering place called *La Vacelle*, [probably *La Vaisselle*], about four miles on, and breakfasted after midday, although the whole property was not that length. As we were contriving how to get on to the next water, the best way we could, the canoe men fortunately met us, which enabled all hands to effect the *pose* completely ; and here we are, within three short miles of the River. With the exception of the first four hours to-day, the road was passable, but many of our pieces were most awkward, such as our *taureau* [pemican in bags] that were made almost round, and to mend the matter, in parchment skins, so that to keep one on the top of another was next to an impossibility. [One on the top of another, for *two* pieces of 90 lbs., is the ordinary portage load for each man.] It would appear that the canoe men had a most miraculous escape yesterday. The guide's canoe, with himself and three men, were within an ace of going to perdition over one of the most formidable cascades they had to encounter. The navigation is excessively bad and hazardous. We have been very fortunate in the weather of late.

Friday, 5th.—Fine day again. Without encountering anything remarkable, we all arrived at the upper end of the portage by eight ; the road was good, and we had but three loads over and above the *charge* of each man. The canoes requiring a complete overhauling, the men washing and mending their shirts and trowsers, and otherwise much in want of a little repose, the Governor has given the rest of the day for that purpose, and he is himself writing a few letters ; one of them for Mr. Hunt of St. Louis. In the afternoon we amused ourselves shooting at marks, playing the flute, bag-pipes, &c. A half-breed of an Indian we have had from the Fort returns to-morrow morning with the canoe from the other end of the portage. In the course of the afternoon Doctor Hamlyn and myself took a stroll down to the first cascades from here, where the water has worked its way into the rock in a remarkable degree, and the whole of the country above this barrier, as far as we see, indicating a strong proof of the edge not giving way to the water many centuries ago, and, of course, forming a higher fall than is the case at present.

Saturday, 6th.—Made an early start, and commenced with the line, which continued, except when we could not help it, till breakfast time.

Dined above what is called *Pointe Grève de la Grande Prairie.* [This is the nearest *déchiffrement* that I can make of this, another unfortunate French name. Some may say it is of no importance ; but it is of importance, in that no traveller here may question our veracity and fidelity. It is truth, not a mere " traveller's *tale*" we would give.] At half-past four, fell in with two Indians of the Chicanee tribe, from which we got a little dried meat. They had beaver, which they mean to trade at Trout Lake. This tribe is at variance with the Beaver Indians, and do not like to visit the establishments of Peace River. Mr. Smith, again, is for supplying them from a small house on the head waters of the South branch of McKenzie's River. I believe at this moment some of them visit another of the New Caledonia Posts on Conolly's or Bear's Lake. They seem to deserve a house [trading house] somewhere, for their country is rich in beaver. A fine encampment to-day, about two leagues above the two rivers where we saw the Indians. Weather pleasant.

Sunday, 7th.—Resumed our journey this morning a quarter before four. Belair's River on our right at seven. Mounted the Grand Rapid about nine, and breakfasted. Clear Water River on our left at eleven. Round Island at one p. m. Hill's Gate in face of rock [or gate in * * * * of rock —the writing is blurred and faded, and impossible to make out,] on our right about five. Encamped at Bernard's River (named after our guide in consequence of his falling in the river with the Governor this evening) at half past six. [Note by Ed.—In disembarking from large canoes, passengers have generally to be carried from the canoe to the shore.] The mountains, this afternoon, assume a stupendous appearance. (*a*) Snow on summit of several of them. Saw vestiges of Indians along the river, and heard a shot in the afternoon.

Monday, 8th.—Started late. At another Grand Rapid by seven, and at Finlay's Branch (*b*) twenty minutes after. There we saw twelve to fifteen Indians, who seemed to have beaver, but have very little appearance of good living. We gave them a little ammunition and tobacco. On enquiry they told us they were not in the habit of visiting any part of the waters of McKenzie's River, they being an immense distance off, (and yet there, before their eyes, were "Waters of McKenzie's River.") Arrived at Little Forks about eleven, and encamped on a fine dry beach on the right hand, about the usual time.

(*a*) See Appendix LVIII.   (*b*) See Appendix LIX.

In the afternoon, met three more Indians that were at the house. (The nearest trading post, "McLeod's Fort," *i. e.* McLeod's Fort on west side of the R. Mts.) They left Mr. Tod and two men there yesterday.

Tuesday, 9th.—Fine day, breakfasted at nine. At La Prairie by one, River la M—— at three, and at the *Grand Remou* before sunset (*Remou* backwater). Encamped about a league above. Saw a number of geese in this part of the river.

Wednesday, 10th.—Passed *Pointe la Cache* at seven a.m. Peace River diminishing fast, (*a*) and entered Black Water Creek at three p.m. which is very low indeed. Encamped at entrance of *Lac la Loche* very late.

. *Thursday, 11th.*—Started early. Lake took us half-an-hour this morning. Entered Little River by right hand branch, which is very shoal, and the canoes in consequence, had to be handed over in many places. Saw fresh tracks of two large reindeer. Killed a goose. Put ashore ; changed, (*i. e.* dress), and breakfasted within 200 yards of the Fort, and just before we entered Trout or McLeod's Lake. Of course we took Mr. Tod unexpectedly. He and his two men were on short commons, their fishery having been very uncertain throughout the summer. Baptiste la Pierre dispatched with letters to Stuart's Lake about noon, and will, in all probability, overtake an Indian that left this in the morning on same message from Mr. Tod.

Friday, 12th.—Remained here all day, preparing lading. Got a few remarkably small white fish (*b*) in a net this morning. No potatoes this season. [Cultivation neglected, probably.] The Indians of this place are twenty-six, exclusive of the Chicanees, and not counting those about Finlay's Branch. Last year they gave about two thousand beaver, [a large return for such a place—Ed.] and this season promise to do equally well. [Here follows a report in all detail, of a case brought before His Excellency, as Judge, of a case of assault by one man on another, under suspicion of tampering with his wife. The verdict—for His Excellency seems also to have been chosen as Jury—was, *Scoticé,* "not proven," but with a powerful recommendation to the accused [*à la* Lord Kenyon, who was, of all Judges, the most severe in cases like this, of *crim con*] not to try that sort of thing again ; and by way of "earnest," a small penalty was imposed, to wit ten shillings, payable as *solatium,* under the benign doctrine of the Scotch Law, *i.e.* Law of *New* Caledonia, in such case made and provided—which money was at once tendered, but was indignantly

---

(*a*) See Appendix LX.   (*b*) See Appendix LXI.

rejected ; whereupon, says the report, " it was made over to another, to buy liquor at the depot :"—on the principle, probably,—also Scotchy :—

> " When neebours anger at a plea,
>
> And are as wud (angry) as wud can be,
>
> It's ae the lawyer's cheapest fee,
>
> To taste the barley bree."   BURNS.

The " beauty " of the Judgment, in its pre-eminence from the top of the Rocky Mountains, whence delivered, was, that it pleased not either party, and, not a little, frightened both out of their impropriety and evil doing in their respective ways, and on all, had a most wholesome moral effect.

> " Most rightful Judge ! "
>
> " Most learned Judge ! ! "
>
> *Shylock, Merchant of Venice.*

" His worship "—winds up the report—" begged their attention, man and all of them, to a proper and correct conduct."]

Saturday, 13th.—Having laid up in Mr. Tod's store, 9 bags of pemican, a keg of sugar, a tinnet of ham and tongues, and a keg of sundries, with two small bundles, the whole for the purpose of being sent for by the people at Stuart's Lake as soon as possible, we made a move at half-past five, every man with a piece, including the provisions, viz :—

1 keg Madeira Wine	La Course.
1 bag Tongues	Delorme.
1 Cassette, McD. and H	Anawagon.
1 Paper Trunk, Governor	Martin.
1 Cassette, Mr. McGillivray	Larante.
1 bag Biscuit	St. Denis.
1 Bed, Messrs. McD. and H	Houle.
1 keg Port Wine	Lasard.
1 *Cave* (Travelling Case)	M——
1 Piece (two tents)	Charpentier.
1 Basket	Hoog.
1 Pemican	Desguilars.
1 Cassette, Governor	Nicholas.
1 Bed	Tomma.
1 Pemican	Peter.

Clothes bag, dried meat, shoes, two skins.... Guide.   Cooking kettle, tea kettle, saucepan, gum....Piper. Guns, great coats, &c., &c., &c....Servant. [The men go in couples to assist each other in taking off and putting on loads.]

Thus loaded, we cannot be expected to get on quickly, for the road is exceedingly bad, no transport of any consequence having gone on here for the last three years, and no improvement or clearing away made on the road.

Arrived at first Lake before seven, and at second by half-past eight. Breakfasted. Off again by eleven, and reached Long Lake about four o'clock. Total distance, say eighteen miles. The last half of the way very oad. Plenty of water all along. A fine day.

Sunday, 14th.—Moved off as soon as we could conveniently see. Long Lake took us but an hour. To Round Lake another, and by eight we arrived at the east end of Carp Lake. This year the road is good, however the ground we came over along the Lake till half-past nine a.m. was very indifferent. To the *traverse* was equally bad. This took us three hours on a very frail raft, which being effected in safety, all hands were treated with a bumper of Port Wine, and we resumed the journey at four. Met a Canadian and four Indians about five. Rode on another hour, and encamped at a small lake on our right, in what is called the *Brulé.* [Burnt wood district.] Guilbault and the Indians proceed to McLeod's Lake for loads to-morrow morning. Had a round on the bagpipes, to the great astonishment of the natives. Distance to-day fifteen miles.

Monday, 15th.—Before we parted from Guilbault and followers this morning, we gave about 25 lbs. pemican to put into *cache* until their return, as their provisions from the Fort are not adequate to the journey. Arrived at River *La Cache* in one hour and a half, and at Half-way Creek in about the same time. Came but a short way further, and breakfasted at the edge of a small lake to the left. Drizzly rain the whole afternoon, but throughout the rest of the day increased to heavy showers, which lasted until we encamped on a small prairie(*a*) on Salmon River. Point of the woods took us two hours, and from there to White River half as long over very fine country. The rest of this day's work took us two hours more, and we encamped at four p.m. drenched to the very skin, after performing a journey of twenty miles.

Tuesday, 16th.—Did not start before six o'clock. Good walking in the morning. Left *Lac des Morts* and another small one on the left hand, and arrived at Carrier Lake to breakfast, expect a few that missed their way, and followed a track that led them three miles to the eastward at Beaver Lake. They joined us in the course of the forenoon. While waiting for them there, two men—Indians—met us from the Fort. They, of course, continued their route to McLeod's Lake. An hour after resuming our journey after breakfast, we bent our course to the right, to avoid the very bad road along a bay in Carrier Lake, [whose outlet debouches near Fort St. James,] and crossed a small inlet on a raft, which took us an hour. Here we again met a Canadian and four Indians with two more horses. They, in like manner, proceeded to McLeod's Lake, and will we trust be able to carry everything. To-night we encamped within twelve miles of the Fort, and have three or four Carriers about us. The bagpipes pleased them to admiration, as well as the bugle, but it was the musical box that excited their astonishment most, especially when it was made to appear to be the Governor's Dog that performed the whole secret. Came eighteen miles to-day.

Wednesday, 17th.—Morning cloudy, and appearance of rain. Our horses not found till late. In the meantime, however, party with their loads commenced their march. Overtook them by nine, and about an hour after, at the last Lake, within a mile of the Fort, halted for breakfast, and changed [dress.]

The day, as yet, being fine, the flag was put up ; the piper in full Highland costume ; and every arrangement was made to arrive at FORT ST. JAMES (*a*) in the most imposing manner we could, for the sake of the Indians. Accordingly, when within about a thousand yards of the establishment, descending a gentle hill, a gun was fired, the bugle sounded, and soon after, the piper commenced the celebrated march of the clans— " Si coma leum cogadh na shea," (Peace : or War, if you will it otherwise.) [Note by Ed.—Though in a sense, a Highlander (Rocky Mountain) and the son of a Highlander in native heath born, I must confess myself unable to grapple such vernacular, and must beg pardon, if in blundering, I offend. I have often heard my father say, that in the multitude and variety of Indian languages, he had to deal with and in the Columbia—and on the Pacific Slope, they are numerous and *radically* varied as the " hundred and one" (fifty odd, I believe) tribes that live, or lived there—he never found the *Gaelic* to fail him at a pinch, as a " universal language."] " The guide, with the British ensign, led the van, followed by the band ; then the Governor, on horseback, supported behind by Doctor Hamlyn and myself on our chargers, two deep ; twenty men, with their burdens, next formed the line ; then one loaded horse, and lastly, Mr. McGillivray [with his wife and light infantry] closed the rear. During a brisk discharge of small arms and wall pieces from the Fort, Mr. Douglas" [Note by Ed.—"Mr. Douglas," afterwards Sir James Douglas, first Governor of British Columbia, to whom, very largely, British tenure in those then bloody wilds is due. He was an officer eminent for his skill, energy and daring, (and his compeers ranked high in those qualities—for the " service" then, there, was one essentially militant, and extremely perilous—I say then, but refer more particularly to the ten years immediately preceding the date of this march to the time of " Si coma leum cogadh, &c.") The journals and letters in my possession, of my father and his numerous correspondents Chief Factors and Chief Traders in charge of different trading districts throughout the whole Pacific slope, from furthest north to the then American boundary, 41° 47′ North Lat. or about that, are full of accounts of fights with Indians, and ever against fearful odds : I refer more particularly to the years of 1822, 3, 4, 5, 6.] Proceeds the Journal—"Mr. Douglas met us a short distance in advance, and in this order we made our *entrée* into the Capital of Western Caledonia. No sooner had we arrived, than the rain which threatened us in the morning, now fell in torrents.

Mr. Connolly, [the late Chief Factor William Connolly, of Montreal,] had not arrived, nor had any word been had of him since the 24th ultimo, then but one day on this side of Kamloops. A letter was forthwith addressed to him by the Governor, and two men were kept standing at the gate until the shower should be over, ready to start with it down the River, when, all of a sudden a canoe appears on the Lake, and in about twenty minutes, we had the infinite satisfaction of receiving Mr. Connolly on the beach, amidst a renewal of salutes from the Fort.

He left the Pacific on the 23rd of June,(a) and we left Hudson's Bay on the 12th of July.

We are now on what may be called the Height(b) of Land which forms this part of the Continent of America ; and it is singular to remark, that without any previous appointment, we should arrive here within two hours of each of other, say at 2 and 4 p.m., and singular also is the coincidence that the salmon, in its annual ascent for spawning, has just, last night, made its appearance ! !

Thursday, 18th.—The fresh salmon at this place is not yet in sufficient quantity to give all hands a good meal, and, of course, recourse is had to a little remaining of that of last year, and the dried carp of last summer : doleful fare to be sure !

In the course of the day, Mr. Yale, and the loaded canoes with the rest of the outfit, arrived, having left one behind which was broken to pieces in one of the rapids below this ; the property will be sent for soon. Now that Mr. Yale is here, it is decided, that as far as Alexandria, he is to accompany Pierre La Course and three men that we send off to-morrow for Thompson's River, to commence building a boat there immediately, to take us down to Fort Langley. Wrote to Mr. Ermatinger, [late Chief Factor Francis Ermatinger,] on this head, and in like manner to Mr. McDougall, that the men might be furnished with horses, and pushed on without an hour's delay.

Friday, 19th.—The quantity of Salmon yet caught is very inadequate to the demands of the day. A few, say from 10 to 15, are taken in the twenty-four hours in 4 or 5 nets belonging to the Fort, and perhaps as many are got from the natives. Geese and rabbits are also procured at this season, which reinforces the table not a little. Weather wet and disagreeable ever since our arrival. Mr. Yale and the four men went off this afternoon in two small canoes, and I may as well say, in canoes too small. The Guide is directed to fall to and put the only two large bark canoes here in the best possible condition to descend the river with to Alexandria, where arrangements will be made for the march. We receive Wocan, the Interpreter, and four additional men here, and can afford to spend a few days longer on this " communication " than was originally intended, so as to give time to the boat builders at Thompson's River.

Saturday, 20th.—Weather still continues the same. The principal Indians of the place have been sent for, and introduced to the Governor as the Great Chief of the Country. After exhibiting before them our various musical performances, &c., to their utter " amusement," an address was made to them through Mr. Connolly and the Linguist, in which the Governor laid great stress upon the conduct of the Carriers (*a*) of late. The affair of Fort George 5 or 6 years ago, is in the recollection of every one in the Country, and which passed unnoticed till this summer, when one of the murderers visited the village of this place, and was destroyed by Mr. Douglas and six men, on the spot. [There is a little obscurity here, but I cannot clear it up. I take it that it means that Mr. Douglas with six men, walked into the village or camp of the Indians harbouring the

(*a*) See Appendix LXVI.

culprit, and then and there "did justice" in the premises. Mr. Douglas was just the man to do so righteous a deed, and with those similarly situated throughout the country, it was the regular practice of the day, to meet all exigencies of a case, at all personal risk.]

The event excited great consternation in some, and indignation in others. The Indians to whom he was on a visit [the "village must have been some little distance off,] thought it incumbent upon them, in self defence, to claim for the relations of the deceased, some property for them in indemnication for their loss, and accordingly they all assembled, and made a clandestine entry into the Fort, and insisted upon getting a blanket.

The death [murder] of Duncan Livingston, one of the Interpreters, is another affair that created violent feelings amongst the Whites this season. In April last, while he and another man were on their way to the Babine [Country North] beyond the portage, he, from some motive or other, was murdered by Indians of Simpson's River in the most brutal manner. Wacon, the Interpreter of this place, shot one of them, and another has been killed by the natives themselves since. The Governor could not do less than deprecate such proceedings. He represented to them how helpless their condition would be at this moment were he and all his people to enter upon hostilities against them. That a partial example had been already made of the guilty parties, but that the next time the Whites should be compelled to imbrue their hands in the blood of Indians, it would be a general sweep ; that the innocent would go with the guilty, and that their fate would become deplorable indeed. The war on the sea coast (a) this season was also represented to them in the most formidable light. [Mr. McDouald had a sharp touch of that afterwards]—and that it was hard to say when we would stop ; never, in any case, until the Indians gave the most unqualified proof of their good conduct in future. [Note by Ed.—The Governor—the late Sir George Simpson—was, though not tall, say about five feet seven at most, of rather imposing mien, stout, well knit frame, and of great expanse and fulness of chest, and with an eye brightly blue, and ever a blaze in peace or war, and with an address which ever combined the *suaviter in modo, et fortiter in imperio.* His was, indeed, on such an occasion, an address to strike awe on his hearers. During the forty years that he ruled the great British North American wild, with all its untamed savagism, and conducted —for he ever regulated every detail of the trade—the affairs of the Hudson's Bay Company, he proved himself the " proper man in the proper place," and few indeed, if any, there could have been found to fill it so well. He entered into the work when all was chaos. That was in 1821-2, immediately after the final struggle of the two great Fur Companies, viz. : the Hudson's Bay Co., and the old North West Co., and even in 1828, the year of the present expedition, the " war" that for years had been carried on from Lake Winnipeg to the Pacific and Artic sea-boards, between these two Companies, involving the red man, had not quite died out, beyond the Rocky Mountains, in· so far as the Indians there were concerned. There had been, in the quiet shades of Fenchurch street, London, a coalition of the giants contestant, but it took time to bring it home to the minds of those rudest natives, about and beyond the Mountain. Hence the need of the present *great trip* across the continent. *A most important mission ;* and one essentially of peace. I must apologize for the length of this note, and hope that its pertinence to the fact now touched on in narration, will sufficiently excuse it.]

The chief that headed the party which entered the fort in the summer was pointed at with marked contempt, and it was only Mr. Douglas's intercession and forgiveness that saved him from further indignities. At the close of the harangue, the chief had a glass of rum, a little tobacco, and a shake of the hand from the Great Chief, after which the piper played them the *song of peace* [the Gaelic name is not given, but of course, from the very soul of the strain, and all Indians have a " soul for music," the song must have been profoundly appreciated.] They dispersed, to appearance quite sensible of all that was said to them.

Letters arrived from Fraser's Lake in the afternoon. The salmon is there in great abundance. [Note by Editor—Near bye, is a lake which has its outlet to the ocean by Simpson's River, which is much shorter, say by two thirds, than the Fraser River from Fort James to its mouth, some five degrees south. *Sea* fish on this summit plateau is a striking fact, and would seem to indicate not only accessibility to ocean for railway from the east, but even a special facility, but of this more anon.] Mr. McDonell was to come himself, but it would seem that a relative of the Indian that was killed here, immediately preceded them, [Mr. McDonell and a man of his fort, probably,] and on the first opportunity fired a gun at Mr. McDonell, which carried a couple of balls within a few feet of him, and in consequence he cannot leave his fort in charge of one man now.

Sunday, 21st.—Raining still. No word of our canoes from McLeod's Lake. Two of the fort men proceed there to-day with four horses, and a small assortment of goods. Letters arrived from the Babine, and Mr. Pambrun, in like manner, gives a hopeful account in those streams. Our men commenced repairing the canoes.

Monday, 22nd.—Late last night, Guilbault, and the four carriers that accompanied him, arrived with their loads, as did also, in the course of this forenoon, the two that followed him on the 16th, but Roy and party cannot be expected for a day or two yet, in consequence of their being out of provisions, and one of the Indians coming on ahead light for some, and who immediately returned. All hands after the canoes. There is difficulty in finding bark to suit our purpose. Rations to men, twenty eight small white fish, or two small salmon, or fourteen dried carp when there is no dried salmon of last season ; of the latter, they generally get four per day. [Note by Ed. This, I believe, is far above the average, fifteen pounds of white fish, equal, say to twenty pounds of carp, and to ten pounds of salmon, being, throughout the Company's country, the ordinary " fish ration," but then, it is to be borne in mind, it is, to use an American term to the point, fish " straight." The meat ration is " 3lbs pemican."

Tuesday, 23rd.—Canoes finished. Weather continues fine. Intended to be off early to-morrow morning had Roy and party arrived to-night. Mr. McDonell came in to-day, accompanied by an Indian boy. This is a gentleman I have not seen since 1803 ; he has been rather unfortunate in the Fur Trade, and his health and constitution are much impaired now in New Caledonia. He has the permission of the Governor to leave this side [of the Rocky Mountains] in the spring, and has also the assurance of a more comfortable berth on the east side.

Wednesday, 24th.—Fine clear day. Roy and party arrived at noon, and in twenty-five minutes after we were off, with the usual compliments of the garrison. To the river took us fifteen minutes. Here the Carriers of the Fort are settled, and have very extensive barriers for taking the salmon in the very entrance of the lake, but the quantity taken as yet is very limited indeed, and great apprehensions are entertained of a year of scarcity again to New Caledonia. Made eight leagues to-day.

Thursday, 25th.—Started before daylight. In still water till five. Breakfasted at head of rapids eight miles above the Small Forks, which is formed by the junction of Fraser's River. On the very point formed by the two rivers, a *chevreuil* deer [roebuck] was about taking the water

for the east shore. We bore down upon him immediately, and as he was
retracing his steps up the bank, he received a general discharge of ball,
buckshot, and beaver shot, which brought him down a few yards in the
woods. We landed at a camp on the opposite shore for fresh salmon,
which we got, and, to our surprise, the greater part of a moose buck just
killed. Left Forks at twelve. Encamped at six, about an hour's march
above the main Forks.   [Note by Ed.—The other " Forks," the " Small
Forks " first alluded to, are on the western prong of the Fraser, while
the lower " Forks "—about, I estimate, forty miles lower—are at the
junction of the Eastern Branch with the Western Branch. The Eastern
Branch is, in fact, as generally recognized, the main stream, and has its
source near Yellow Head Pass, as indicated in my Letter No. 7 of the
series (signed Britannicus), in June, 1869, in the Ottawa *Times*, under
the heading, "The Canadian Pacific Railway, an Imperial Necessity."
The Western Branch, probably the smaller and shorter of the two, has
its source in Fraser's Lake, or rather a small lake, a little, say about
twenty-five miles north of Fraser's Lake, within about a hundred miles,
in air line, from Pacific slope, near " Naas Harbour." From the
plateau, *i.e.*, of Fraser's Lake, and its surrounding lakelets, two main
streams to ocean, offer way, viz., Salmon River, and a large branch
of Simpson's River. Their descent, from a height say of about two thousand feet, must, of course, be very rapid, but from the fact that Salmon
are caught in their upper waters, as appears from the letter of Pambrun
above reported, (and Pambrun, in the course of trade and communication
thereabouts, at that time, must, I assume, have been on this same plateau),
they are, to that height, evidently *salmon streams*, with no intervening
fall beyond the limit of highest salmon leap, viz., fourteen feet. The
only other ports in those latitudes, down to the mouth of the Columbia,
were at the foot of our great Western rock slope, or revêtment wall, viz :
Fort Langley, at the mouth of the Fraser, and shortly afterwards, Fort
Simpson, in Observatory Inlet. The sole communication in the trade
of these coast posts, was by the Company's schooner's, and shortly
afterwards by their service steamers. The trade on the coast was confined to the coast tribes, those at the foot of the wall, and had no communication with the *inland* trade, which was conducted by the old route
from Fort Vancouver on Columbia River, *via* the Columbia, Okanagan,
Kamloops, and Fort St. James. The coast range was, no doubt, a
formidable physical obstruction, but had it been desirable for trade to
surmount or penetrate it, by some one or more of its 'gorges, the Com-

pany would have done so, but it was their policy of keeping the trade back, off the touch of American opposition on the coast, that, I believe, was the real wall—Chinese wall—of separation. But to proceed with the journal.] Indians here and there along the river, with *verveux* [sweep nets] at each lodge. Fine navigation all day.

Friday, 26th.—Thick morning. At Forks by five. A few minutes before, left ruins of Fort George on our right. This branch, which, properly speaking, is the continuation of the Fraser's River, receives Salmon River about twenty-five or thirty miles above this. It is navigable to *Tête Jaune's Cache,* as our communication with the Saskatchewan with the Leather, is this way (*a*). Breakfasted ten miles above West Road River, which we made at half-past eleven. This stream, though celebrated in the travels of Sir A. McKenzie, from the circumstance of his following it up, when he started off to the sea, has hardly a drop of water in it. Passed River de Liards (on left) at four, and a few minutes after, the the "Clayey" Pyramids, on each side. Quesnel River half-past five, also on left. Encamped three miles lower down.

Saturday, 27th,—Breakfasted at second point above the house. At House by ten. [Note by Ed.—This place, "House," is Fort Alexandria, as appears by letter, *now before me,* dated "Fort Alexandria, Western Caledonia, 8th March, 1828," from "Geo. McDougall," then in charge, and addressed to my father. The incident is a small one, but under the circumstances, is, I think, worth mentioning. Mr. McDougall's letter contains much of interest as to the country, and states amongst other noteworthy things, that the scarcity of salmon the year previous was *unprecedented* (he was then at Fort St. James,) where he arrived in November, from my grandfather's (Pruden's) Post (viz, Fort Carlton on the Saskatchewan). The statement in the letter that he left Carlton on 20th August, and arrived at Fort St. James, in November, shows that he could not have gone by the very "long about route by the Columbia," but by the Yellow Head Pass, a line of route forming the *shortest* side of a triangle, and by all means the easiest, as appears from the fact of his sending, shortly before that, by the same route, his sick brother James, (powerless in limb) to the East side for medical aid, and who returned by the same route, meeting the Caledonian party at Cranberry Lake.] The two McDougalls are here, besides Mr. Yale, who, with his party, arrived on the 22nd. They started in a few hours after, with each a horse, and

(*a*) See Appendix LXVIII.

must be at Kamloops to-morrow. Had everything prepared by four, and made a start shortly after. There are four of ourselves, five men besides Indians, and five loaded horses. Came about four miles, and encamped on second little stream from Fort. Mr. Yale and fourteen men leave this to-morrow in two bark canoes to the Forks of Thompson's River, where we trust to meet them in twelve days. Salmon again appear scarce in this part of the country.

Sunday, 28th,—Had our horses collected early, and were on the move a little before six. Passed the last of the two steep [word omitted here] about eight. In a few minutes the canoes hove in sight, put ashore, and breakfasted with us at half past eight, at what is called "Head of Rapids;" distance from House twenty miles. Governor very unwell. He embarked with Mr. Yale, to accompany him to the division of the roads, three or four leagues lower down. Here we left the river at two. Encamped at four on Current River, which falls into the main stream within two miles of first small Lake. Athna Chief with us: he came from "*Le Barge*," since Yale passed.

Monday, 29th,—Gregoire, who came with us to last nights' encampment returned in the morning with a few spare horses we had, from the Fort. The Athna Chief had a note for a small present from Mr. McDougall. Started at six. Passed two little rivers during the morning, and breakfasted on main stream at eleven. Resumed the journey at one, when we immediately crossed, and re-crossed in an hour after. Continued on North side. Another little river at two. A Lake, half a mile, at three. Encamped at four within a league of Long Lake. Governor still unwell. Road very good indeed. Killed a few ducks.

Tuesday, 30th,—Off this morning at five, having the horses in camp before daylight. Reached end of Lake at eight. Crossed to south in fifteen minutes. Came to an ordinary encampment on small river running from a Lake about half a mile round, but did not stop ; continued for an hour longer, main river vanished. Breakfasted at Salt Lake, which afforded ourselves and horses but shocking bad water. Near this place had a chase after a large grizzly bear which soon took to the woods. Point of the woods took us an hour, and in another we arrived at a large stream which flowed to the left. Crossed it immediately at beaver dam about one o'clock, and continued on North bank for three hours, which brought us to another lake, a mile of which we made this evening, and encamped before a heavy shower came on. The river we came along to day has all the appearance of beaver, fresh. Dams are all over it. Course, for the last two and a half days S.E. Governor much better.

Wednesday, October 1st.—Started at half-past five. Lake took us till eight. Breakfast at half-past nine on main river. Off again about noon. Came to another Lake at two. Encamped at the other end at half-past four. In woods whole of afternoon. Tom killed a goose. While struggling with his horse, Doctor Hamlyn had his gun entangled, and his shot accidently went off without doing any harm to those before him.

Thursday, 2nd.—Wind and rain during night. Started at usual time. First half of road, good, along a chain of small lakes, but the last part was hilly and rocky. Came to a small Lake half a mile long, and breakfasted. The lakes to-day seem still water. The afternoon journey was a gradual ascent on what is called the Mountain. Here also passed several small ponds and a number of swamps, that must be "very bad going" in spring and very soft weather. Encamped at height on a little M...... between two little lakes. Governor quite recovered. Journey very pleasant. [This must be the height of land between North River and Fraser. Ed.]

Friday, 3rd.—Started at six. Began to descend about eight, continued so for a whole hour coming down to the first small stream at foot, which we crossed, and in an hour more got to the *traverse* of North River. Here we found Lolew, the Kamloops Interpreter, who left a canoe and two men from the Fort a little below this, early in the morning. Laprade arrived with the canoe about noon. In about an hour after, the horses, alone, and most of the men, crossed, and continued the journey on the other side over a piece of very bad road : ourselves with three men and the baggage embarked at three, after an harangue with the few Indians there, and got to the proposed encampment in two hours, where the land party joined us soon after. Cinnitza, the Chief, stopped with us, and had an order for a small present at the Fort. Our course in this river is south, and will be so, it is said, until we arrive at Kamloops. River pretty large, and no strong rapid.

Saturday, 4th.—Horses could not be collected early. Governor and three men in canoe again this morning ; rest of us accompany the Horse Brigade. At Barrier Village by eight. Crossed two rivers in succession soon after. Got to the Stockades about eleven, when the whole expedition again breakfasted, surrounded by the Indians of the Barrier, who are anxious to see the Governor, who made them a speech, and sealed it with a foot of tobacco to each, the Chief getting a more liberal supply.

The road thus far to-day, is not bad, and to the House, is uncommonly fine. At the Pines we all took horse, and with our flag flying formed a respectable cavalcade. Did not arrive at the House [Kamloops](*a*) before dusk. Pipes played, and much firing on both sides. Courtapolle and a few Indians at the House. Much to our satisfaction, we find our boat is finished, and which was begun only six days ago. Mr. Ermatinger and four men here. Mr. Dears and six men at Fraser's River for Salmon.

Sunday, 5th.—The Governor expressing a desire to see *Nicholas*, a man was sent for him. We await the return of the bearer till twelve o'clock. Mr. Ermatinger is to be continued here for the season. Mr. Dears arrived late from Fraser's River, but the men will not be here for a couple of days. He says Mr. Yale and the canoes passed on in safety, the day before he got there, and that he did not see him. A good deal of salmon at the bridge. Indians about, anxious to see the Governor.

Monday, 6th.—Laprade arrived about noon, but did not see *Nicholas*, he being out hunting. The Indians, immediately after, were directed to assemble in their own Hall, [Hall, as in all main posts, appropriated to Indians,] and there, the Governor, in due form, attended by all the Gentlemen present, met them. He, of course addressed them, and at some length, adverted to the propriety of behaving well among themselves, and exhorted them never to be guilty of theft, murder, or of any inhuman deed towards the Whites. To strengthen this argument he produced, read, and translated to them two letters sent by the Indian Boys at the Red River Settlement Missionary School to their parents at Spokan, and the Kootanais Country [places immediately South and S.E. of Kamloops, in the Columbia Country.]

The Shuswhaps listened to the contents with apparent interest, and of course promised to behave themselves accordingly. Lolew is engaged for three years as Interpreter: He and two " bouts " accompany us from here. Boat in the water at four. Soon after, embarked in *full puff*, leaving Courtapolle, Tranquille and the others small presents according to their rank and good behaviour.

We are now sixteen in all. Blowing very fresh indeed, and only came to the entrance of the Lake [seven miles below Fort.] Horses are sent from this place to meet us at the Coutamine from 20th to 25th, in case we do not go round by the Souud [Puget Sound.] For the same reason letters are sent to Fort Colville, Walla Walla and Vancouver [All these are chief posts on the Columbia River, the lowest—Vancouver—being about ninety miles from the mouth of the Columbia, and being the Port

---

of Entry, for the whole trade on the west side of the Rocky Mountains.]

Tuesday, 7th.—Having the Lake [Kamloops Lake, Thompson's River] before us, we started this morning as early as four, and did not reach the other end [estimated at from 15 to 17 miles] before a quarter to eight, notwithstanding that it was a perfect calm, and that we had twelve paddles in the boat. At the breakfasting place, remained an hour and a half with Indians. Ran a number of minor rapids before we got to *La Rivière Bonaparte* by one p.m. A little below passed a dangerous one, then three *dalles* [natural slides] which were perfectly smooth, and below which was *Rapide de la Grosse Roche,* which ought to have been taken on the left side, as we took in much water by running close to the rock on the right hand. This we ran at a quarter before two. In half-an-hour made Point Observation, or Wood Point, and in succession *Rapide Croche,* and Long Rapid at a quarter to four. To Coutamine River Forks took us another half-an-hour. McDonald's Encampment at a quarter to five, and in fifteen minutes more, put ashore for the night. It is in this neighbourhood that the Indian suspected of killing two of our horses lives. We have a search for him. He disappeared, and we are as well pleased. His name is Babiard.

Wednesday, 8th.—Off at six a.m. Three strong rapids to Nicumine: ran all without examination by seven. Visited all the rest for about a mile which comprehended four principal ones : the second and last very dangerous indeed. In the latter we were nearly swamped, for in three swells we were full to the thafts, and the danger was increased by the unavoidable necessity of running over a strong whirlpool while the boat was in this unmanageable state. Left this place at eight, and in another hour, after running the worst places, arrived at the Grand Forks, where we were much gratified to find Mr. Yale and our people quite safe and well. *This meeting is rendered still more interesting,* FROM THE CIRCUMSTANCE OF BOTH PARTIES DESCENDING RIVERS THAT WERE NEVER RAN BEFORE. [That is to say, *dangerous* parts not run before,] *and that were always considered next to impossible.*

The Indians that were assembled around the camp in such a novel scene being addressed, and the necessary arrangements for the prosecution of our own voyage being made, we started at one p.m. The Governor took his own canoe with eight men. A gale of wind that commenced three days ago seemed to increase this afternoon, consequently our progress was slow and hazardous. Although none of the rapids from the Forks to this place [McDonald's Dalles] are bad, yet we found them dangerous,

and did not perform the distance—4 miles below the Forks,—before five
o'clock. The boat went down the dalles, but the canoes not daring to
follow, was brought up again on the line, and here we are for the night
in a very bad encampment. The Indians hereabouts are about the usual
number. Their salmon fishery must be over, for not one is there to be
seen on their stages now. One [blank in M.S. accompanies us to the
sea : he has been there already. Here, in like manner, were made anxi-
our enquiries after villains that shot three of the Kamloops horses, when
Mr. Ermatinger and party were here for salmon ten days ago.

Thursday, 9th.—Weather moderate. Off at six, when we could well
see in the *dalles.* Governor embarked in the boat with me, and Mr.
Yale took his place in the canoe. Were soon in a long rapid, with a
small stream from the mountains on the right hand, at foot.

Good run to Allitza River on the same side, which we passed at eight
leaving the other about half way. Strong whirlpools below, which forced
Bernard to return and descend on the opposite side (the right.) From
this place, where we were detained three quarters of an hour, we had a
good run over a current of great velocity to the Sandy River, which we
made about nine, and breakfasted. Gumming, and running *dalles* till
twelve.

This is a bad piece of navigation. Here also, we took on board Latzie,
one of the Coutamine Chiefs. Five hundred yards lower down made use
of our lines, and at the foot of the same cascade, on right hand, carried
the canoes, and here were detained repairing, gumming, &c., for two
hours. The boat ran the portage part of the river, but required great
skill and vigilance. Many Indians about us here, but they behaved well.
The boat had a peep at the next place before the canoes came on. This
place we call the Gate Dalles. Very good going down, but should a line
be required to ascend, it will be a task of some difficulty to pass it on
either side. First rapid of another nature at three : then a smooth piece
of a few miles before we came to Mr. Yale's river, which has also a strong
rapid at its mouth, and to get down, the guide was induced to land the
passengers and two men out of each canoe. There was some delay before
they could ford the river. Left this place at four, and in twenty minutes
arrived at the head of the Fall. Examined it minutely. Boat undertook
to run right down mid-channel : did so, keeping rather in eddy to the
right, and did not ship more than we had on one or two occasions already
experienced. No passengers and only eight men were in the boat. The
canoes crossed to the west side, and made a portage over a good sandy

beach of about two hundred yards. Not an Indian there. After a detention of about three quarters of an hour, we again pushed on, and at a
quarter past five, encamped in a small sandy bay on the west side, surrounded by detached rocks for fifty or sixty paces back, behind which, on
both sides of the river rose mountains almost perpendicular, and of incred-
ible height, well clothed in the lower part with Pine, Fir, and Cedar
trees.   A number of the natives soon gathered about us, and continued
to arrive from below throughout the night, with large flambeaux to direct
their steps.

They were perfectly quiet and inoffensive.   Our two Indians from the
Coutamines or Forks, smoked with them till midnight, although the
strangers did not seem passionately fond of the Virginian plant.

Our course to-day is about south.   The river made no great bends, but
owing to occasional delays, and being often in strong eddies and whirlpools, our distance cannot be estimated at more than fifty miles. *At least
half the distance, the river is deeply imbedded in the solid rock,* and the
other half is of bold rapids, with, however, plenty of water all over. The
mountains in no part of this day's work, recede from the very edge of the
water.

The natives seem to use but few canoes, for in places we have observed,
that instead of gaining access by them to a particular stand near the
water's edge to watch the salmon, they contrive *by many ladders* to
descend from a considerable height, and return by the same hazardous
communication with the fish.   Foot paths, if any, are very imperfect,
and I believe, that when they do travel from tribe to tribe, they scramble
on along the rocks and face of the mountains at some distance, the best
way they can.

Friday, 10th.--The river in no part of this day's work was more than
a hundred and twenty paces, and often not quite half that in width.   In
getting our boat and canoes in the water this morning, it was remarked
that the river had risen three feet during the night. The little rain we
had could not have been the cause of this.(*a*)   Started at broad day-light,
and in twenty-five minutes came to head of Simpson's Falls, where the
river is choked up by a most solid rock of about half an acre in extent.
Examined it along the west shore, but conceived the run on that side
extremely dangerous, and owing to the immense rocks all over, to carry
was impossible. The East lead was then determined upon, crossed, and

(*a*) See Appendix LXX.

run without landing on that side, by the Guide who rushed on with his
bark canoe, and a safe arrival below was effected, but not without much
risk in the whirlpools against the enemy [the rocks] that hung over us. (a)
The boat followed, but did not suffer by the eddies so much, as it did by
being swallowed into the swell of the Fall, out of which the utmost power
of twelve paddles could not keep it. The second canoe having the advantage of being behind, came on with greater precaution. A few hundred
yards below this, we came to the next and last run, which was steep but
uniform. Then the river began evidently to assume a different form. The
water was settled, the beach flatter, and vegetation more profuse.

At eight passed a large camp on right, which could only have been
abandoned a few weeks before. Behind it sprang up a lofty, rocky Mountain in the shape of a cone, and being the last on that side, we celebrated
it by the name of Sugar Loaf Mountain. Continued our descent till half-
past nine, and landed for breakfast, which did not detain us forty minutes,
treating our people with some of the *taureau* we had at Dunvegan. None
of the small rivers to the left attracted our particular notice.

At a quarter to two, passed the mouth of " Lilliwhit " River, [now
Harrison's,] a stream of some size, as is indicated where Mr. F. Ermatin-
ger arrived on its banks, a day's journey west of second Peselive Lake in
August, 1827, and as appears in his report to me on the subject,
"Thompson's R. Correspondence 1827-28." Another River, half-a-league
below, on opposite shore, which comes from the neigbourhood of Mount
Baker, rich in beaver according to our Guide's account. At half-past
three o'clock, MET THE TIDE FROM THE PACIFC OCEAN. Work's river on
right at five. Head of McMillan's Island at seven, and arrived at FORT
LANGLEY(b) precisely at eight, where we found Mr. McMillan himself,
Messrs. Manson and Annance, and twenty men. [Note by Ed. I have
Mr. McMillan's private letter to my father, dated from Fort Langley,
January 21st 1828, reporting the cutting by him, on 1st August, 1827,
of the " first stick for the Fort." He mentions Messrs Manson, Barnston,
and Annance as being with him.]

Saturday, 11th.—This Establishment was begun in the early part
of August, 1827, with the above complement of people and the assistance of the schooner Cadboro, and as many more during the space of six
weeks. The Fort is 135 feet by 120, with two good bastions, and a gallery
of four feet wide all round. A building [blank in MS.] feet long, of three

---

(a) See Appendix LXXI.   (b) See Appendix LXXII.

compartments for the men, a small log house of two compartments, in which the gentlemen themselves now reside, and a store of about [blank in MS.] feet are now occupied, besides which there are two other buildings, one a good dwelling house, with an excellent cellar and a spacious garret, a couple of well finished chimnies are up, and the whole inside now ready for wainscoting and partitioning, four large windows in front, one in each end, and one with a corresponding door in the back. The other is a low building with only two square rooms and a fire place in each, and a kitchen adjoining made of slab. The out door work consists of three fields, each planted with thirty bushels of potatoes, and look well. The provision shed, exclusive of table stores, is furnished with three thousand dried salmon. sixteen tierces salted ditto, thirty-six cwt. flour, two cwt. grease, and thirty bushels salt.

I am thus particular with the Establishment of Fort Langley, as it is my own lot to succeed the present "*Bourgeois*" [officer in charge,] who forthwith accompanies the Governor in Chief to the Columbia, and thence in Spring to York Factory, and perhaps Montreal. The complement of men is reduced to seventeen, and Mr. Yale 'takes the place of Mr. Manson.

Here of course ends my Journal of the voyage. The Governor is furnished with a copy of it.

APPENDIX.

NOTE I.

YORK FACTORY, according to Thompson, "Astronomer to the North West Company," and who surveyed the country from Hudson's Bay to Pacific, is in Latitude 57° 1' N. and Longtitude 92° 26' W. of Greenwich, and which by comparison with other observations of that "objective point," is evidently as correct as we require, viz., as a definite starting point of measure of the route we propose to follow from Hudson's Bay to the Pacific. The Lat. and Long. given in the Navigation Tables. [I am citing from that Standard work, "*Norie's Navigation*,"] are respectively N. L. 57° 0' 3". Long. W. of G. 92° 26' the difference probably being owing to the fact that the *Sea* Point at the mouth of Haye's River is four or five miles east of York Factory, and that, perhaps, the southern point of the River's mouth was taken for observation on the *Coast*.

York Factory, or "York" as it is put in some of the older maps, has

a history. In times past, [viz., from 1697, immediately after the treaty of
Ryswick to 1713,] it, as *Fort Bourbon*, gave fierce battle to the "Governor and Company of Adventurers of England trading into Hudson's
Bay," [the Charter name of the Hudson's Bay Company,] and incarna-
dined those Artic Waters in a strife that was brought to a close only
by the Treaty of Utrect, in 1713; under which, the French " ceded" the
whole coast, and Hudson's Bay, to the English, and who, of course, have
held it ever since.

In the autumn of 1830, on my way to take ship passage to London, it
was my good luck (for the present nonce) to see it, and then—only two
years after the Canoe voyage of Governor Simpson—it was, I believe, just
as it was when he started thence on his " flying trip across the continent ;"
in which, we now propose to follow him.

It is long since I saw York Factory, but still I remember it pretty
clearly. Emerging from the sombre woods of the world in which I had ever
lived, and after the long and dreary crawling boat voyage of many days
through the gloomy wilds of rock, swamp, and dark waters, we had just
gone over from Norway House, the, to me, new thing, with its tinned
roofs, shining in brighest ray, burst in the distance on my unaccustomed
gaze, like a city of burnished siver :—beautiful exceedingly !—a St. Peters-
burg of America, but with its St. Isaac's (that matchless dome !), of silver,
instead of duller gold : the back ground and framing, was illimitable
swamp ; and towards the furthest east, water,—the calm, dead, summer
sea—sky bound. It was a striking sight, but not to be compared with
the grandeur (sublimity would be the proper term, for there is ever
something elevating in the sight of large masses of ice,) of what I saw in
the ice world of Hudson's Straits, a little further on.

York Factory is situated some miles from the mouth of Haye's River,
on the North side, and ships cannot approach within ten or fifteen miles
of it, or even more, according to their draught, so flat and shallow is the
shore,—western shore—of Hudson's Bay ; and it is so throughout, the
same difficulty existing at Moose Factory, six degrees further south, as
well as at the mouths of all the rivers that side of the Bay.   Hudson's
Bay is in fact, a huge " Sea Mud Pool."

Mr. McDonald in his Journal, speaks of the " Garrison " of the place.
It was, of course, in mere *persiflage* of the moment he used the term.
There had been, however, not very long before that, during the North
West troubles, a large force there, sometimes amounting to "ninety men;"
I say " ninety," for I have read the statement from a reliable source.

These were there not to defend the Factory however, but to be sent forward as soon as possible, to the interior, where all the fighting was going on; but in York *Factory*, and which was merely fenced, and not picketed or palisaded, like a Fort with a wooden wall, fifteen feet high or more, and had no enemy to fear, the only vestige of a garrison was the mounted Artillery, four handsome eighteen or twenty-four pounders, on the high bank in front of the Factory, or Company's storing place. Gun firing is, (or was during my time there) a favorite mode of salute throughout the whole North, and therefore, I thoroughly believe the statement as to the parting cannon shots, for good luck, so joyously referred to in the Journal. The "fourteen commissioned gentlemen" then being *there*, was a specialty, which will, hereafter, in a note on another subject, be explained.

Note II.

" *Light Canoes* "—specially made and adapted for speediest travel. I saw those, the very ones spoken of, at Norway House, on their passage up. The Governor's was the most beautiful thing of the kind I ever saw ; beautiful in its " lines " of faultless fineness, and in its form and every feature; the bow, a magnificent curve of bark, gaudily but tastefully painted, that would have made a Roman rostrum of old hide its diminished head. The paddles painted red with vermilion, were made to match, and the whole thing in its kind, was of faultless grace and beauty—beauty in the sense of graceful and perfect fitness to its end.

This class of canoe is, [or rather was, for I am speaking of times now somewhat old,] generally known under the name of "North Canoes," from the fact, that on the arrival of the largest kind of canoes used in the trade, viz., those which used to be dispatched [and that until very lately] from Lachine, on first open water, to Fort William, Lake Superior, and which were called " *Canots du Maitre*," had to be exchanged, or left behind for smaller craft, half the size, and such as could be portaged from that point upwards. The Canot du M. was of six fathoms, measured within, and the C. du Nord about four, more or less. The ordinary crew for the former was sixteen or eighteen, and for the latter eight or nine. The larger could stand any storm in Lakes Huron and Superior, but it was ever the habit of voyage to avoid the encounter as much as possible. Their ordinary load was one hundred and twenty pieces of ninety pounds each, say five tons, with men, and passengers' baggage. They always carried passengers, say from four to eight or even more in case of children. I never heard of such a canoe being wrecked, or upset, or swamped;

they swam like ducks. If overtaken, as was often the case, in a long *traverse* from point to point, or across large bays in the big Lakes, the heavy "*parla*" [red canvas oilcloth] used to be thrown over the goods as a storm deck, and then, skilled strength and pluck, with the trusty bark, did the work. The average rate on still and calm water was from five to six miles per hour, but the Governor's rate was always a little more. Ninety miles a day was his average on some routes, i.e., down stream.

In a small canoe with three men, I have myself, done 98 miles, [distance scaled,] in twenty-four hours, including six portages, and three hours for sleep. The Governor, I have no doubt, has often beaten that, for he ever had the best of canoe-men, Iroquois, and any extra " Canadians " who could keep up with them in quickness of stroke. [60 a minute at times,] and otherwise be up to *their* mark in the work.

Note III.

"*Governor in Chief.*" Governor in Chief for the Hudson's Bay Territories. There was a Governor of Assiniboia, Red River Settlement, which office however, was ostensibly confined to the administration of Government—such as it was—in the Settlement, but had nothing to do with the *Trade* proper. This designation of attribute and duty however, does not apply in all strictness to the earlier Governors of Assiniboia, who were generally, if not invariably so for a time, Chief Factors in the service of the Company. The supreme Governor was the one of the London Board; but for the regulation of the trade, the working of its machinery, a Governor was appointed by the Governor, and Committee of Directory in London, for their Territories, who, with a Council of " Commissioned Officers," meeting at a central point, which was Norway House, at the head of Lake Winipeg, was the only constituted body for conducting the business in the Territory, and it was only as the head of this body, and with certain special power *in eundo*, that Mr. Simpson, [afterwards Sir George,] was at this time Governor in Chief.

Note IV.

"*Commissioned Gentlemen.*" Chief Factors and Chief Traders and successors to the original Chief Factors and Chief Traders, all partners, under the Deed Poll of 1821, on the coalition of the two contestant Companies, the Hudson's Bay, and North West. Forty out of the hundred shares of the whole concern were specially reserved for such partners, whose contribution was in skill and work done. They received " commissions" from the London Board, and were hence called "commis-sioned gentlemen."

They were now in York Factory, assembled from their different, and some of them from very distant posts, in Council. Norway House—the old Norway House, had recently been burnt, and not being yet rebuilt, the Council had met in the meantime at York Factory. My father was then building up the new Norway House, and had all ready for the Council next year, where they met, and have ever since used it as the business capital of their whole country.

Note V.

"*Cassettes.*" Trunks made of best and well seasoned pine, and made as strong and light as dovetailing, grooving, iron binding, and good work-manship can make them. The stuff throughout, is three quarters of an inch thick. The dimensions are two feet four inches in length, and one foot four inches in width and depth, and beveled on top to the extent of nearly an inch, leaving the sides about fifteen inches and a quarter deep, of this depth, the cover [made to fit closely to a lap in the body of the box] takes from four to three and a quarter inches. Of the "Cassettes" used in the country, this is the largest size, and the smallest does not vary more than an inch, in any way. They are well painted, and are proof against any accident but fire.

"*Case.*" Travelling Case, a *multum in parvo*, with compartments "for everything" that man may need on the voyage for his table and camping, save the main stores and bedding. Every compartment is well lined with some soft stuff; good baize generally. The liquor bottle department par-ticularly, containing precious "medicinal" for the numerous and inevi-table accidents on the voyage or journey, is generally most carefully looked to in the packing. In the multiplicity of utilities in "the Case" the traditional "pin" is there, and almost, also, the "anchor."

"*Baskets.*" Also with compartments, and suitable tin cases, for meats, sugar, and other groceries; those for meats being invariable finely per-forated on the top. Here also, that indispensable—the frying pan, which by the way, should be made with a good strong hinge—has its place, to wit on the top of the contents. The basket is made of strong willow, and amongst Hudson's Bay people, is strong enough for any service or accident.

"*Kegs Spirits.*" For the "men," are generally of five gallons, if I re-member aright; the "spirits" are the "best of rum—genuine Jamaica," in fact, every thing the Company, its officers, men, and customers get, is of the *very best* quality, and the Indian, in trading, knows the fact. The common Indian gun of the country, is made with special excellence for use, on special order of the Company, and for both services, shot and ball, and for trueness and general service in the North American Wild, there is no gun like it.

"*Beds.*" Oil skin, buffalo, and blankets.

"*Agrès,*" also spelt Agrèts, is the voyageur word for "outfit," and is applied also to equipment of canoes &c.—rigging is our word for it.

"*Pactons.*" Pacton is the French-Canadian word for bundle, and in the North, is applied more particularly to a bundle tied up in a manner to be easily carried on the back. The carrying-strap—a most important instrument in that world of portages, is very carefully made, as failure in it is ever, or rather would (for I never knew one to fail) ever be a little disastrous. It is made of a strong piece of stiff tanned leather, about four inches wide at the broadest part, and about eighteen inches in length, to this are strongly sewed strips of equally strong leather about ten feet long, and from two inches to half an inch, tapering, in breadth. The best "*colliers*" are made with the broad part, and two or three feet of the string part, all of one piece, and the rest of finer leather for tieing.

Note VI.

"*Two o'clock in the morning.*"

"*Star levé.*" (Contraction, very contracted, of *C'est l'heure à se lever*) as the voyageurs call it. And poor fellows, they are always ready, and cheerily jump up to their work, and out of their heavy and *so well earned* sleep of four, or at most five solid hours in the twenty-four. They know nothing of an "eight hours" movement, and dont dream of it : *eighteen* hours is their labour time, and that of the hardest.

Two o'clock is the usual starting hour in Summer in those "Higher Latitudes," and from eight to ten the camping one, and yet the work is the very hardest that any men anywhere undergo ; and the pleasure of it is, that there is never, or at least very rarely, any push, and certainly no Legreeism in it.

Note VII.

"*On the Line.*" Line by which the canoe is hauled up stream, when the current is too strong for paddles or poles. From this point upwards, the current of Haye's river is, if I remember aright, much swifter than it is about a hundred miles and more further up, where, however, it is more broken. In fact, at this part on the slope Silurian of the Hudson's Bay Basin-rim, the descent is as that of a *dalles.* A descent of over three feet per mile in the river flow generally requires the line.

NOTE VIII.

" *Rock.*" There are a number of portages in pretty close succession a little above this, if I remember aright, and at one of them, the boats also have to be hauled over. There is a regular roadway for the purpose, with round sticks a few feet apart, for rolling the boats on. A couple of crews can haul over one of them in a trice. They are called " five ton boats," and look large enough to be that ; and moreover, they are, neccessarily, very strongly built.

NOTE IX.

" *Red River Settlement,*" at this time, drew all the supplies by this route. And what little it did export, such as tallow, had all to go that way. The Settlement must have had immense internal resources, a country rich enough to feed and clothe itself, to survive such isolation. My father, with two men, constituted the whole settlement *on the spot,* during one winter, when the Colony was dispersed by the enemy. Out of the débris, they gathered seed enough to start cultivation the next spring.

NOTE X.

" *Painted Stone.*" " *Portage de la Roche Peinturée,*" is at or near the " height of land " on this route. The actual " height of land " here, as everywhere else that I have seen, read, or heard of, of the great Laurentian Range, or Ranges from Labrador to Athabasca, a distance of over two thousand miles, is ever a flat, or flattish. I have found it so, above three hundred miles almost directly north of this (Ottawa City) where I measured it, as best I could, as an amateur in that way, for it was sport alone that drew me there. However, with the means at hand, viz., a good thermometer (for ascertaining heights by the " boiling point,") and with other instruments, and besides that, by careful measurement of the heights of all falls, cascades, and principal rapids on the way, viz., the St. Maurice River, to a point (Weymontachingue) about two hundred miles from its mouth, (that was before the river was scaled by Mr. Bignall, of Quebec, but I determined the point by careful astronomical observation,) and further, by careful observation of the general character of the current, I arrived at an estimate which would place the height in that meridian, at nearly one thousand feet. From that point I canoed up the main stream, till I came to a flat which I was told (and which seemed to me likely) extended to the Hudson's Bay waters.

From the head of the waters on the Hayes' River route, flowing into that river, to Sea River, which is outflow of Winipeg Water, is but a step, and that, over a flat, as is shewn by the Journal before us. I allow ten feet, (an excess I believe) for the difference of level between where Mr. McDonald reports, having struck "Black Water Creek," and its mouth, on Sea River. From that point to Norway House, is a distance of about forty miles, with a considerable current to be stemmed part of the way : I know it personally, for I saw it constantly during the four years I was there. Allow for that, a descent from the Winipeg level, of say, 5 feet, and we have the "height of land" very little above the level of Lake Winipeg. The level of Lake Winipeg (from 628 to 630 feet) as determined by a number of authorities.—See blue book, *passim*—is about the same as that of Lake Superior, and is probably assignable to the same cataclysm. A few miles below Black Water Creek, viz., about 70 miles, to judge from the map, (Arrowsmith's) before me, the "height" actually runs under water, viz., at where Winipeg, under the name of Nelson River, dashes on to the sea. From that point, the height slowly rises till at or near the Methy Portage, on the route to Athabasca, it again culminates with the same marked feature of flatness—a flat of several miles there and about there. Of the "height" there, we will speak when we come to that part of the route, as the route itself, in this canoe voyage is our chief index on this point.

NOTE XI.

Aitchemanus.—I have given the word precisely as I find it written in the journal. My idea is that it is an Indianization of the term *Each man his own way*, which I find applied to it in Thompson's Report. What gave rise to the name was the fact, that when the precious and ever trusty beavers that used, with their dam works, to keep open this high-way on the "height" of land, were killed, (a ruthless deed, for they had ever been cherished, and tamed in a way,) the dam or dams gave way, so that several driblets of water courses, and sometimes scarcely any at all were left, and to make a way, it was necessary to "stop-block" all the water-courses save one, and in that manner, *each man had to make his own way*. Sometimes, it would seem, as in the present instance, all the water-courses were stop-blocked—probably to gather water for the boats. In the present instance, the season being a remarkably dry one, as appears from the journal, and the water short, it was necessary to carry *all*— *canoes* and all—over, instead of making, as was usual, a "demi-portage,' viz., carrying in whole or in part, the freight, and floating the canoe or boat.

NOTE XII.

" *Sailed up Sea River.*"— This is the last stage of the route from York Factory to Norway House. Let us survey it as best we can. The recent expeditions from England under the Imperial Authorities, under the conduct of Captain Palliser and others, may have given details on this subject, but they happen not to be within my immediate reach, and, in any case, for all practical purposes at present, the report, thoroughly reliable, of Mr. David Thompson, " *Géographe de la Compagnie du Nord Ouest*," as he was styled in the books of the time, is " authority " that cannot be questioned. Mr. Thompson was an intimate and esteemed friend, and known to me as one incapable of a misstatement, and was a man of most conscientious carefulness in all things, and no less so, of course, in his profession, to which he was passionately devoted. He did more for a correct mapping of our great North and North-West from Hudson's Bay to the Pacific than all others put together. It would be well to have his valuable field notes, now in the keeping, I believe, of some one of our Departments of Dominion Government, printed at public expence, for they are now, from age and character of hand-writing, fast fading out of sight. As to the particular part in question now before us, I happen to have a report, printed in an old *brochure* in French, and which being rare, and of some possible value in the present juncture of general enquiry as to those so long and studiously "darkened" regions—"darkened" from the world's eye of enterprising intelligence—I shall give it in full :—

[TRANSLATION.]

Measurement of the Distance and of the Stations between York Factory and the Colony of Lord Selkirk : by David Thompson, Astronomer and Surveyor of the North West Company.

York Factory is situated in latitude 57° 1' N., and longitude 92° 36' W. The rivers are freed from ice in the latter part of May or beginning of June ; yet the banks remain covered with ice and snow till towards the middle of June, at which time the navigation is at length really open. Snow begins to fall about the middle of September, and by the twentieth there is generally ice and snow along the river edge and banks. No canoe can arrive at Red River, starting from York Factory, later than from the 1st to the 16th of September. The canoes or boats, &c., which navigate (" *qui navigue*,") from York Factory to Red River, do not ascend Nelson River, but Hayes' River, on which the factory is established. [Note by Editor,—the Nelson River route had been abandoned, and also the Churchill River one, both being too difficult.]

Geographical
Miles.

River Hayes [from York Factory.]...............................   52

 For about eight miles one can ascend this river aided by the tide, but all the rest is very strong current (*courant violant,*) which requires haulage by the line.

Main River.—Canoes from the South ; is also called *Nipegon Steel River* ; it only admits of haulage...........................   27

Hill River,—Very strong current, and haulage necessary to the first Fall...   32

From Fall to the upper part of the river...........................   30

 This distance is but a succession of banks of sand, impetuous currents, broken rocks, cropping up to water level (*à fleur d'eau*) ; it requires twelve portages, independently of partial discharges and disembarkments at several places.

Lake Swampy (Lac de la Savanne)...............................   7

Jack Tent River (Rivière aux Brochets).—With much current, and five portages...   10

Knee Lake (so called perhaps from its form, or from its shallowness)...   47

Trout River.—With current at several places (*plusieurs courans*), and two portages...   13

Holy Lac (Le Saint Lac.) [Note by Ed.—Certainly well named, a beautiful large sheet of water, with a bordering of comparatively low shore, and with no heights in view ; like a summit lake. Oxford House is finely situated on it.]...   30

Several small streams ("Ruisseaux,") and *small lakes* with five portages...   50

Each away man's brook. [Note by Ed.—It is so, in English, given in English in the French report.] There are there, ten beaver dams, which are carefully kept up. In dry seasons, the way being as dry as a threshing floor, it is necessary that voyagers wait until the streamlet ("Ruisseau,") to be navigated, be filled by the return of the waters   28

Hare Lake (Lac au Lièvre) discharges itself into the "Saskatchewina" or *Saskatchiwine*...................................   7

River Saskatchewina or Saskatchiwine. [Note by Ed.—I give [the name precisely as given in the Report. The *Cree* name

is *Kisiskatchewan* (swift current) and in the *old* books and
papers is written Siskatchewan.]   Continual portage......   35
Play Green Lake...   14
Lake Trempy—[Note by Ed—Winipeg]—distance measured
   on the east side, which is shorter than the west...............   300
Red River to the Forks.   [Note by Ed.—Forks by junction of
   the Assiniboine River.]...   40

_____

From Y. F. to Forks R. R...   725
Note by Ed.   Deducting the last three distances stated, for
   Norway House is between Y. F. and Play Green Lake, say   357

_____

We have as the distance from York Factory to Norway
   House   368

These being geographical miles, we have the distance at, say, 430
in statute miles.

Norway House is in latitude 54° N. and longitude 98° 10′ W. as determined by the several observations by competent scientific men who have
passed there, the gateway or wicket of the north, and final starting point
of some of the Arctic Expeditions. The distance in air line between these
determined points is about, and scarcely, 250 statute miles, and even the
higher of the above figures, viz., 430 would give a liberal allowance for
divergence.   All of that distance, save, probably fifty miles, is seaward-
slope, and allowing an average ascent of a foot and a half to the mile,
(which is above the general river average of *pente*, the world over), we
have an indication of height of source—height of land—corresponding
with what we have already advanced on that head.

NOTE XIII.

" *Jack River House* "—but ever since known as Norway House, and,
in fact Mr. McDonald elsewhere in his journal refers to it generally, if
not always, under its proper name, Norway House.   The old Norway
House, which was situated somewhere else, at the head of Lake Winnipeg,
had been burnt, as before stated, and a new Norway House, with an
extent of buildings adequate to its position as the seat of government of
the whole north, from Hudson's Bay to the Pacific and the Arctic Ocean,
had just been built—a two year's good job—at, or near " Jack River."
My grandfather (maternal) Chief Factor Pruden commenced it, and my
father built the most of it, and finished it, when in charge of that district,
(the Norway House District) and it was just completed, when the arrival,

now narrated, occurred. The " House " is as large as an ordinary sized village. Built somewhat like a fort, but with only a comparatively slight projection at the ends in the front facing the river, in place of the " bastions " of the regular forts. The inclosing wall was a huge board-looking picket fence, perfectly close, from twelve to fifteen feet high, and formed a square of about a 150 yards on a side, with two gates, one in front, and the other in rear. This enclosure contained two large stores or warehouses, each about sixty feet in length, one on each side on entering, and in the middle of the square, was the main row of buildings over 200 feet in length, and comprising the dwelling of the officer in charge, a large hall forty or fifty feet long, for the great general council, and a number of spare rooms for members attending council, and for the Governor, there was a special house, if I remember aright, there was also a building for clerks, and the kitchen (a large affair) and other buildings, offices, workshop, the whole on the same scale—all these were in the " bounds,"—beyond, in rear, and on one side, at some distance, a quarter of a mile or so, were the men's houses, two long buildings, sub-divided for families. Boat building formed no small part of the work of the place, and that also, had its little building yard and place. Such was Norway House, in its fresh new face, as I saw it made, and left it, over forty years ago. On it, or much of it, as on all things, I have no doubt, that Time has passed his effacing finger," for those were the *golden*, specially golden, times of the great Fur Monopoly of British America North, and all was gladness in the hall there, then. I thus give, at some length, this sketch of a Hudson's Bay Trading Station, *Ab uno, omne disce—mutatis mutandis.*

On the Saskatchewan, amongst the fierce Indians of the Plains, and on the west side of the Rocky Mountains, the trade, in those times, but more especially for some years before that, was ever at the cannon's mouth, and in the case of my grandfather Pruden at Carlton, (which he built) and was then the chief place of trade with the plain Indians, it had, *ex necessitate,* to be carried on at and through the little wicket at the gate, flanked and guarded by the bastions with their dreaded " wall pieces " loaded and ready. Men there, then, carried their lives in their hand, and life, nowhere in the North, was a sinecure.

The situation of Norway House is, if not romantic, one to please the eye rather than to repel. It rests, snugly under the shelter of a high rock towards the east and north, and in fact under sheltering eminences, not high however, all around, the country about, being, what is called, a " rolling one " instead of a hilly one. In front of the " Fort,"—for I must give it some name more intelligible than " house,"—and fully twenty feet down the bank, is a small bay, on the right of which (facing northward) is a small rock hill, about eighty feet high, with a spur which narrows the channel to about a couple of hundred yards in width, and where the current (Sea River) seaward, is from three to four miles an hour, at that particular part, and for about 400 yards, the course below that immediately below, becoming lacustrine.

The country around is principally of rock, in knolls, swamp well covered with pine, spruce, and cedar (possibly), and there is considerable dry ground for such latitude and meridian. The trees, chiefly, are pine, good and of different kinds, spruce, and birch, white and red or black even, if I remember aright. There was, at any rate, a good birch "sugary" in the neighbourhood, but of which, of course, no sugar came, but most unexceptionable "*syrup*," and "it went as well." There may have been maple, probably was, viz. the northern kind. The trees are of "fairly large size," a log "seventeen inches in the "but," the smaller "but," being not an impossibility, or rather, *was*, for it was of the *virgin* forest, there, I speak.

The staple (food) of the place is fish—sturgeon, royal, of full one hundred pounds now and then, I believe, and "Jacks" (pike), and that "life" of the Laurentide country, the ever delicious, *never* cloying, and ever cherished, beautiful whitefish of our far northern lakes. Not only the establishment (a couple of hundred mouths on an average), but all the brigades, from the Rocky Mountains, McKenzie's River and Red River and York Factory, on their arrival there, where they had to remain a little while, were fed there on fish, and it sufficed them.

NOTE XIV.

"*Chief Trader McLeod, and Dease.*"—John McLeod, "senior," (my father), and Peter Warren Dease, afterwards Chief Factor, and for whose most efficient services in conducting the management of the then last Franklin land expedition, and that known as "Dease and Simpson's," and which completed the survey of our Arctic coast from the McKenzie westward, and also added much to our line of discovery on the east, from the Coppermine R. eastward and northward, was offered a knighthood by the British Government, but with that modesty which was part of his noble nature, he refused it. I knew him well. I have his autographed copy—his own—of the report of that most perfect, or one of the most perfect, in its working and results, of Arctic expeditions, and the least costly. The zeal and thorough knowledge of every necessary detail in material and working, on the part of the Governor for the Territories,

viz., Governor Simpson, and the "happiness" of his choice in selecting
Mr. Thomas Simpson (a relative), a gentleman of high educational attain-
ments as well as of great natural ability, contributed, no doubt, much to
the success of the undertaking, but it was unquestionably mainly due to
the special qualities of the two officers at the head of it, and who carried
it out throughout.

I shall have occasion hereafter to cite a passage or two from the report,
as best authority, in certain explanation or information called for by the
argument involved in this writing. I say report of the work, but it is
really only Mr. Thomas Simpson's admirable journal. Conscientious,
intelligent and painstaking, his statements as to astronomical observations,
taken by himself, and other matters bearing on our subject, are
thoroughly reliable.

In the crowd on the bank, so graphically described by Mr. McDonald
in his journal, standing beside my dear old father, (a sturdy Highlander,
snuff box in hand, and with countenance beaming in conscious pride of
his work well done, viz., the " Capital " just built—the New Norway
"House, behind him), I (a little fellow yet in his units), was a " gazing
spectator," intensely interested, and to this day, I remember the scene as
if it now flashed before my eyes.

On the signal hill of rock, from a tall Norway Pine shaft, floated the
" grand old Flag." From the " hollow rocks "—the world of rocks—all
around us, awoke the wild echoes, by " the bugle," " set flying." Then
the grand thunder—skirrl of "the bag pipes," with their " Campbell's
are coming, hourray! hourray!" or some such " music of our mountain
land," loud droned out to the very vault of heaven. And then—as a
cadenza of soothing, gladdening, exquisite charm—the deep and soft and
so joyously toned voices of those full throated *voyageurs*, timed with a
stroke—so quick—of glittering paddle blade, singing with such heart
their "*La Claire Fontaine*," or some such loved air of *their* native land—
our own land, let us say.

All this music, in the rapid, in the deep rocky gorge, mellowed by the
waters, and a little by distance, entranced us, in a sense, for, for a while,
we could but listen—the canoes, from our position in the bay, being out
of sight—but when the Governor's canoe, with its grand high prow,
rounded, and brightly painted, flashed out of the dark rock " at the
point," into our full view, and gracefully turned into the little "port" at
our feet, the heart seemed to swell with admiration and delight at the sight.
Never; never, had anything so grand and splendid, and delightful withal,
been seen in those primitive wilds ! and the little world there, especially on

that "bank" that day, was one which, in its unsullied purity of natural taste for the beautiful in nature, and in simple art, could appreciate and enjoy such a scene.

Note XV.

"*Play Green Lake*,"—Is so called from the accumulation (borne down by Saskatchewan current) of a green, brightly green, water weed on certain parts of it, and more particularly at its entrance, or rather at the entrance into it, of Lake Winipeg, at a point which, I presume, is the one referred to in the journal as "Warren's Point," and which, I believe, is also called "Mossy Point." But this is mere conjecture on my part. *Pacho*—the *ch* being sounded as the same letters or *gh* in the Scotch word loch or lough—is the Indian (Cree) word for the weed. Hence the name W*innipi-Pacho*, the big water with the green weed.

This green weed, which to the eye is as scum, abounds in those waters, and, I am told, gives name or significance to our "Winipeg." I spell the word with one n, though perhaps, strictly, according to the vernacular, there should be two. Brevity is the order of this day of shortness and electric quickness, and though sadly failing in the effort (for my schooling is a little old), I shall, kind reader, try my *petit possible* in that way, at least hereafter.

The lake is one of the most beautiful I ever saw; full of bare rocky islets, from which I have seen gull's eggs of every size, from pigeon to turkey, brought to Norway House in small canoe loads.

Note XVI.

"*Grand Rapid*."—This "Grand Rapid," at the mouth of the Saskatchewan, is so fully and thoroughly, in all its bearings, described and discussed in blue book, that I shan't enter on the subject. I feel, however, disposed to take this opportunity, of a word about our great and most interesting Saskatchewan. The name is written very variously. In some of the oldest accounts of it, I find the name spelt Siskatchewan, and if I mistake not, it will be, or would be found so in the old papers (if they could be got at), of the Hudson's Bay Company. Thompson, in his report above cited, writes it *Saskatchewina*, which, I believe, is the true Indian pronunciation.

As to what is, or should be the Saskatchewan, I hold that it has as much right to recognition throughout its *whole* length and grandeur, in its course from the summit of the Rocky Mountains to the Sea, as the St. Lawrence or other lacustrine stream of this continent. In fact, more so, for there is, we may say, no "Big" Lake to break its course, for from the mouth of the river at the foot of its Grand Rapid, to the head of the Lake is but a short distance (about ninety miles probably) without a single stream to intermingle its waters, and from thence to thence to the sea it is, in fact almost wholly, Saskatchewan water. From Norway House downwards, Thompson refers to the current as Saskatchewina (the swift river). I am aware, from maps, and accounts, such as that most abounding repertory "Dobbs' Hudson's Bay," (a copy of which I happen to possess) that the so called "Nelson R." in its course from Lake Winipeg, or Play Green Lake, draws largely from the N. W. by streams debouching into Split Lake, but still the accretion is altogether too small to change the proper name of the main stream. As well, might we call the St. Lawrence, something else, because the Ottawa strikes into it at *Bout de L'Ile*, below Montreal. This would make our Saskatchewan at least two thousand miles in length.

Note XVII.

"*Freeman.*" Name applied to men who have left the Company's service. There are no "slaves"—slaves in any sense—in the country, and there never were, nor, in fact, could be; but some distinctive appellation was necessary to distinguish those in the country, in the service of the Company, from those who were not, and hence the name. No offence was meant in its application, and as to those to whom it was applied, it bore the import of honourable service faithfully done and finished.

Note XVIII.

"*Traverse.*" Crossing by water. In navigating lakes of any considerable size, it is necessary for canoes to be careful in the long reaches, and hence it is that in large Lakes, such as Winipeg, quiet moonlight nights, and early morn, are preferred for the long "*traverses.*" Winipeg is, I believe, the windyest Lake in the world, and the winds, especially the "Northers," are of terrific force.

Note XIX.

The custom is for canoes to stop, in case of heavy rain, and to go under cover. A heavy oil cloth or two, is always at hand ready, for the purpose. The men, as well as the goods and luggage, are ever carefully looked after.

Note XX.

"*Through reeds and long grass.*" This part of the Saskatchewan, viz. : from some distance below Cumberland House to the head of the

Grand Rapid below Cedar Lake is a vast flat of fast accumulating alluvium, the precious earth cream of the great Saskatchewan basin. When the water is high, as it is in June, when the mountain winter snows come, liquid, down, there is not a foot of land to be found in a day's paddle and sometimes more, and then, any hard jutting piece of limestone rock is a luxury.

Note XXI.

" *One dry night, since leaving Norway House.*" Before that, from Hudson's Bay (the wettest part of North America) to Norway House it was all dry weather, so that the very mosquitoes were dried up, to the death. The rain-fall in the Hudson's Bay Basin is very much greater, certainly, than that of the Saskatchewan from Lake Winipeg, westward. I have not the hyetal tables of the regions in question at hand to show the fact, but they are accessible to the general reader, and are, moreover, if I mistake not, in our own blue book of 1856–7–8.

Note XXII.

" *Cumberland House.*" As well determined by the numerous observations of explorers passing that further wicket or doorway to the north, as well as to the west, is in Latitude 53º 57', and Longitude 102° 21' W. and is distant about 190 (one hundred and ninety) miles from Lake Winipeg. It was once a post of considerable importance, in the time of the " old troubles " there, (over fifty years ago), when this and the adjoining the English River District—a fur garden, then—was crowded with the rival traders. Even yet, the post is rich in rats ; the country around being an inexhaustible *habitat* of that most indomitable and conservative of our *feræ.*

Note XXIII.

" *The Guide.*" Governor, or no governor on board, is ever master, *absolute*, of the march. As a class, they are certainly the most trustworthy of men. The present canoe voyage from Hudson's Bay to Pacific, and on waters through real gorges, canyons, with rapids, dalles, cascades, " *chûtes*, falls, &c., and that without a single accident, to life, limb, or property, and without the loss of pin's worth, save a ten cent paddle on a portage, proves their quality. He was, generally, some steel framed, steady and electric eyed Iroquois of Caughnawaga, or, as I believe in this case, was, some old French Canadian *voyageur*, wise, exceedingly, in his own way, and endowed, one would think, with special instincts for his duty. In canoe, he takes the post of honor, *i. e.* of danger and trust, the bow.   Between him and his precious charge, every nasty ripping rock, or sunken stick in the way, the shallow way—for going up stream they have ever to hug the shore—there is nought but the thin birch bark, and its slender lining. He must needs, therefore, watch every inch of the way.   On the other hand, when running a bad rapid, or, more fearful still, a *chûte* with its whirlpools, what a world of lightning calculations and electric force of thought, must fill and flash from that brain and unmoved head, which with its long ebon hair, flashes hurtling in its plunge, like a meteor, through the mists of boiling waters ! On such occasions not a word is said, the steersman, the biggest giant of the lot, takes his " cue " from a sign from the bow's man, generally imperceptible to others not trained to the mystery, and at it they go, as one heart, one mind, quickly, strongly, but ever (and in this the native shows almost a speciality), with a reserve of physical power and nervous energy equal to the occasion. " Stoic," he, never loses his presence of mind.   'Tis *he* runs our steamboats down the fiercest rapids.

Note XXIV.

" *English River or Churchill Waters.*"—The portage into this "system" of waters is the " Frog Portage," which is marked in most of the maps, and which is stated at being only 370 (three hundred and seventy yards) and not to be of any special steepness. The upper, or Beaver River, portion of this Churchill River watershed, intermediate between, and in fact, at flood, overflowing into the Saskatchewan and Mackenzie Red River " systems," is a fine country for a settlement. The soil is good and strong, well wooded, and even heavily, with " magnificent pines," as well as other valuable timber, and is in the " Belt"—" Fertile Belt," that our latest reporters in blue book speak of.   That is true, but I hope to show before long, that in giving their " Fertile Belt," they dont go far enough north and west.

Note XXV.

" *Pelican Portage.*"—Simpson (Thomas) of Dease and Simpson, in his " Narrative " (page 84 of the book a posthumous one), thus speaks of the *Pelicans.*   " A considerable part of the 5th (June) was occupied by the Pelican Portage, and that of the Drowned," [Note by Ed. This must have been about 130 miles north of Fort Chipewyan, on the Mackenzie River.] " The desert-bird, he goes on to say, frequents the first in prodi-

" gious numbers, and the rocky islands, a mile out of the stream, were
" crowded with their white ranks, reposing after their morning's fishing."

Note XXVI.

" *Fort de l'Ile à la Crosse.*"—This is an important post. Its position
is given with great precision, by Simpson, according to observations taken
by him in the course of his remarkable winter journey on foot all the
way from Red River Settlement to Fort Chipewyan, via Fort Carlton, a
distance of " 1277 miles," as given (most truthfully I believe) by him. He
thus speaks of it :

"The Fort " is neat and compact, the surrounding country low, and
swampy. The fishery in the Lake close at hand, yields a constant supply
of fresh and wholesome food, summer and winter ; the little *farm* is pro-
ductive, and the few *domestic cattle maintained, were in excellent condition.*" The Longitude of the place, deduced from three sets of lunar
distances, with stars on either side of the moon, was 107°. 54′. 30″ W.
differing only six seconds from that found by Sir John Franklin in 1825.

The Latitude is not given in the published narrative, but in Bishop
Taché's Sketch of the North West, I find it given at 55°. 25′. and of
course he has taken it from authorities ; it agrees sufficiently near with
Arrowsmith to be depended on. I am thus particular as to this point,
because from it to Fort Chipewyan has ever been, to all scientific research
as well as to commercial travel to the Arctic overland, the one route followed summer and winter, and the route as to distance, measured and
checked in every way, and ascertained with every possible certainty, short
of actual trigonometrical survey, is known almost as the " measured
mile." Simpson gives it at 371 miles (statute), and he walked every inch
of the way with snow shoes, making the road for his men and dogs every
step of the way, in heaviest snow, in mid-winter, in the short space of
ten days, an average of 38 miles a day, when and where, 25 miles would
have been good work. On his return from his remarkable Arctic feats,
which occupied two seasons, he exceeded that.

Note XXVII.

" *Packs.*"—" Packs " are packs, most tightly made by screw presses,
strong enough to make say five hundred mink skins into a bundle, two
feet in length, one foot nine inches in width, and about fifteen inches in
depth. On this, however, I speak with some degree of vagueness, for in

the first place, I was never in the Fur Trade, and secondly, it is nearly a third of a century, since I was in a Fur Post, even casually.

The "pack" differs a little in size and form, according to nature of pelt, skin, or fur, so that a pack of buffalo robes would be larger much than one of mink, or such like small fur. *Weight*, the standard "piece" of 90 lbs. for carrying, is the measure of make.

The McKenzie's River District has ever been a very valuable one, if not the most valuable in quantity, and that, from the fact of there being no opposition, and of its immense extent, reaching even to far Youcan, where as on the North Pole of its new masters, now possibly float the "stars and stripes" of the United States of America. At least they claim it under the Alaska purchase, but whether they should get it, without a recognition of that general principle of law, one of obvious equity, of paying for improvements, and further without a recognition of our *droit de retention* until such payment, is a question of some interest, especially at this juncture. The Youcan outlay by the Hudson's Bay Company, would cover much.

NOTE XXVIII.

"*Cold Frosty Morning*."—On the 7th of August, in the heart of the "Dog Days," is certainly something to make one shudder or sigh, as the case may be, for such clime. For a summer trip, if possible ever by rail, commend me to *Methy Portage*, were the refreshing nerve bracing breezes of the pure, grand, and strengthening, farthest North, without a stop or a break from their ice world, may refreshingly kiss and fan in summer breath the toil worn, or more pitiable still, the care worn brow of Southern humanity.

The fact is, that this is the summit spot, between the Arctic basin on the one hand, and a basin which is almost Arctic on the other—for the waters of the Churchill "system" are but snow just melted from the heights of the Rocky Mountains—and in part also eastward from this spot, from the "Barren Grounds," of the naked Laurentian Primary, of those leafless, bladeless wilds.

From the brow of this height, the northern end of Methy Portage, let us step down, down to those dancing sparkling waters, where first they stop as it were, in their haste to their home back in the north. A thousand feet above the sea they say, is the height of this "pass" from Ocean to Ocean. I believe it, and therefore believe, that even in the "dog days" it is *cold, there*, at times of a morning.

Note XXIX.

"*Mr. Stuart.*"—Chief Factor John Stuart, whose son (Donald) was a fellow boarder of mine, at Dr. Boyd's, one of the Masters of the Edinburgh High School. I saw the old gentleman there, and had an opportunity of knowing his character, and it was one of thorough truthfulness. Besides, in the present instance, in making the statement I am about to refer to, there was no conceivable motive for the slightest variation from truth. He was at the time of the voyage now under consideration, in charge of the trading District known as that of " Lesser Slave Lake," and which extended from Clear Water River or Methy Portage to the Leather Pass *(Passe de la Cache de la Tête Jaune)* and the "Rocky Mountain Portage," or " Columbia Pass," or " Boat Encampment Pass," as the old Hudson's Bay People called it in my day, when I crossed it. In extent it is about four hundred miles from east to west, and two hundred from north to south, say eighty thousand square miles, and is the very Eden of our north. It is thoroughly permeated by numerous streams, such as the Athabasca, McLeod, Pembina and Lesser Slave Lake Rivers, which afford navigaion in every direction. Lesser Slave Lake, about 100 miles long and about 30 broad, at its broadest, lies about the middle of it, but rather towards the north, approaching at its upper end, (where the chief trading post of the District was, I believe, at this time, and may yet be for aught I know,) a southern bend of the Peace River, say within sixty miles of it. It was from this point, say Lat. 55°. 40'. and Long 117°. West, according to Arrowsmith's map, that the letter I am about to cite, was written. The The letter is one of a number collected from every trading district in the whole field of the Company's trade from the Atlantic to the Pacific, and from the American Lines, then 41° (forty-one) 47' N. Latitude on the Pacific Slope, to the Arctic Ocean, and as a report for the Council, and for use of all chief Factors and chief Traders (a business letter) was addressed to Norway House.

The collection is of value, not only to the trade, but as a general report as to everything affecting it, viz., climate, food resources, navigation and general trade communication. A most perfect census also was taken, reported and recorded of the whole country.

Of such is the following citation, and I give it because it is exceedingly little we have of any information from that particular quarter, *one out* of the ordinary lines of travel. In doing this, I violate no confidence or accidental trust. The Company have moreover, no secret to be ashamed of, and though they wisely and properly kept their affairs to themselves, in the present change of matters, it is in their interest as well as that of the public that this information should go forth.

Letter of Chief Factor John Stuart.

Lesser Slave Lake, 10th December, 1826.

"To the Governor, Chief Factors, and Chief Traders." [That was how all those official reports were addressed.] "*Notwithstanding the season is so far advanced there is not a grain of snow upon the ground, and the Lake is as free of Ice as in June.*" Free of Ice as in June ! and yet the place is ten degrees north of this [Ottawa City,] and is almost within sight of the Rocky Mountains. The statement as to the climate accords with Thompson's " April," [April, not May] " 28th, cold blustry morning, came to Slave Lake, partly open and partly sound ice."

Amongst the packs of fur returns, he speaks of a number as being " swans," i.e., skins with swan-down. The Country abounds with deer and wood-buffalo, or at least did then, and I believe does so still. He speaks also of the fine crops of barley and potatoes, raised at places much higher up towards the head of the Saskatchewan, whither he had gone on a visit.

Note XXX.

"*Portage of twelve miles.*"—This is by far the longest portage in the whole Indian country, and by that, I mean the whole Hudson's Bay Territories, and the Territories beyond. Fortunately it is a comparatively level and easy one. I am under the impression that of late years the Company have had animals, horses or oxen, to assist in the work, but I cannot venture an assertion on that point. I find however, in Bishop Taché's admirable *brochure* on the North West of America, a positive statement to the effect, that from the Saskatchewan, [probably opposite Carlton House] there is a " Cart-road to Green Lake." [I was born there.]

From this point to Carlton (Fort) [my Grandfather Pruden's old place, and which he built,] is only about a hundred miles of fine, easy and well wooded country. From there to Red Deer Lake close to the " Big Athabasca, is, in vegetation in its singular force and nature, the rankest part of America, North of the Torrid Zone." These are the very words, applied by Sir George Simpson himself, if I mistake not : A region of sulphur waters, bituminous springs, warmest limestone beds, and full of life, animal and vegetable ; the *veriest* garden of our North West.

The Pine Forest, according to Simpson who tramped the whole route in winter from Carlton to the Fort of Green Lake, begins at Latitude N. 53° 30′ commencing at " Fishing Lake," a little more than half way towards Green Lake from Carlton. From Green Lake to Red Deer Lake already mentioned is the shortest, easiest, and in every respect best route to the Athabasca Region, and even to Athabasca Lake, and is moreover the straightest route, almost in air line to Lesser Slave Lake, and is, when the water is not at its lowest, the best and safest road to Jasper's House, " head of boat navigation," *and to the Yellow Head Pass,* a four day's march or less. A good waggon road from the Saskatchewan, from the Forks or below " Cole's Rapids " or " Coal Rapids " as they are also called, to the bend of the Athabasca, about thirty miles south west of Red Deer Lake *ought to be one of the first public works in that region.* The road would not be three hundred miles in length, there are no large rivers to cross, nor hills of any account to surmount, and it could be made, I believe, for less, much less than a thousand dollars a mile, in general average throughout, much of the route being through prairie. Such a route would supersede the Methy Portage one, even for the McKenzie River Trade.

NOTE XXXI.

" *Poses* of 500 to 600 yards each."—That is the distance between each usual resting places—breathing spells for the *voyageurs* when " carrying " in the long portages. The ordinary load is 180 lbs. in two " pieces," one tied like a " pacton," with the small long ends of the " *Collier*," and which lower piece is made to fit into the small of the back as it were, and to rest on the ilium, or " upper big back-bone " of the hip. The second piece generally some bag shaped thing, or even a barrel or a box is thrown on, and rests as in a hollow, long and convenient on the back between the shoulder blades. The broad part of the *Collier* is put across the brow, the neck is slightly bent, at the angle of most resistance by the neck and spinal column, the legs as well as the body are slightly bent, but just enough for spring, and off, so loaded and trimmed, starts the man at a bound, short but quick, and which even on rough ground up hill or level, he keeps up at a rate on an average of five miles an hour. The littlest men do that easily and I never saw nor heard of one who would touch less than the standard " 180". The disgrace would be killing, and the rivalry, ever lively, of who will carry most, has called forth feats in that way that would make the traditional " porter of Constantinople," hide his diminished head. His "mark " if I remember aright was "600" (lbs. av.) Be that as it may, he could not, I am sure, carry " *Le Grand Canot*," up a hill, and down, as our " *bouts* " do, nor "do" Methy Portage better than our men do or did.

Note XXXII.

" *Reduced to one Trading House.*" During the struggle of the two companies, N. W. & H. B., to secure and to monopolize the fur trade in the country, their " system " was to have " posts" opposite each other, and each would start new posts here and there wherever an opening for trade presented itself.   In other words, the trade was in a way brought to every Indian's tent door, and he was served as a veritable " lord of the land."   The result may easily be imagined.   And when on the Coalition, there was a total change in this respect, the discontent amongst the Natives was very marked, and even yet, at the period of the voyage before us, that discontent had not entirely subsided.

Note XXXIII.

" *The propriety of discontinuing the use of spirituous liquors.*"   The policy of the Hudson's Bay Company is, and has been, since they were masters of the situation, worthy of all praise ; for it is undeniable, that " liquor " is certainly the " most profitable article," *i.e.*, *immediately* profitable article of trade with the Indian.   True, the company, as a corporation, with an existence *future* to look to, may be said to be not in the position of an individual, in the country only for the time (short as possible) to make money—his " pile "—by trade with the Red-skins, and is not subject to the same *temptation*.

There is, of course, something in the argument—but, on the other hand, there is to be said, viz. : That the Company—"a close corporation," if you will, [I mean the old H. B. Co.] was composed of men of high and far seeing intelligence, and from the first effort in 1811, of Lord Selkirk, to settle the country, must have seen, in a sense, those coming events which mark the present hour in their field of work.   *Carpe diem*, was not wholly *their* policy, at least, where humanity to man, the duty of " brother's keeper," dictated, in their good consciences, the " better course."   At the time of the Coalition, or rather in the " trade year" just before it, it is of record— in so far as " record " of such a thing, and under the circumstances (very special), was, or could be possible—that some way or other, at least *fifty thousand gallons of spirits* were introduced, in that one year, amongst the Indians, in, or for trade.   In the first year of the Coalition it was reduced to ten thousand gallons ; that was in 1821-2. In 1825, as I find by the Minutes of Council, at Norway House, for that year, trade in liquor was discountenanced. These Minutes I have, viz., the copy of them, certified, which my father, as Chief Trader, in charge of Norway House District, shortly after that, had, and which had been left for him by his immediate predecessor, my grandfather, Chief Factor Pruden. Such Minutes are, it is true, an *esoteric* of the Company, and even although not improperly possessed of them, I would not, in strict law and honor, be justified in giving them or any part of them to the public ; still, on this point, and in this matter, I have no qualms of conscience. It would have been better for the good name of the Company, in some respects, I think, if they had not been so *esoteric*, and had borne in mind that there was such a thing, and power, as public opinion.

Extracts.

" Minute 108—Indians :—Industry to be encouraged, vice repressed, and morality inculcated. *Spirituous liquors to be gradually discontinued*, and ammunition supplied even to those not possessed of means."

While I have this precious Minute book before me, let me cite one or two more of some relative bearing.

" No. 137. Charles Lafreniere fined £20 ; for *charitable* purposes."

And under the head " *Religious Improvement*," I find the following :

" No. 138. Divine Service to be read Sundays.

    „ 139. Religious books to be furnished.

    „ 140. Immoral habits to be checked. Opposites to be encouraged.

    „ 141. Premiums for juvenile rivalry.

    „ 142. Women and children to be always addressed in English or French.

    „ 143. Parents to instruct their children in A B C.

    „ 144. Officers and clerks in charge of Districts and Posts to take measures to carry these several moral resolves into effect.

    „ 107. *Missionary Society :*—Native children leaving their parents to become attached to this institution, to be supplied in goods not exceeding £3, on account of the Society.

" No. 90. Catholic Mission at R. R. recommended for an allowance of £50 per annum with a supply of luxuries, &c. [The " luxuries " were a little tea, sugar, &c.]

That was when the company was poor, and had not yet recovered from its troubles. Since then, the company, and its Chief Factors, and Chief

Traders have covered the vast field with Mission Stations, and the most thorough missionary teaching in the world. One gentleman alone, Chief Factor Leith, if I remember well, gave ten thousand pounds sterling, to the great cause ; but while many of the company, who spent their lives in the service of the Indians, have given freely of their gold to the missionary cause, it is no doubt to the noble zeal and effective teaching of the Roman Catholic Clergy, ever welcome at every post, as brothers of the Cross in a common cause, that the christian civilization of the North American Indian is mostly due. I am a Protestant, as my father was, but we can bear no other testimony on this point. The priest and the trader have in this case, gone hand in hand ; and commerce has, in truth, in this instance, been hand-maid to religion. For schooling and schools in proportion to population, Red River Settlement has nothing to be ashamed of.

NOTE XXXIV.

" *Delightful prospect down this River.*" Clear Water River. " *La Petite Rivière Rabaskâ,*" as the old *voyageurs* used to call it. Every one who has passed it, and has written thereof, has expressed admiration at the beauties of the scene; and even Mr. McDonald, who, from his journal, seems to have too studiously,—too studiously for our taste at least,—closed his eyes to the living pictures along the way—seems to have been affected here. Captain Back's account of it, probably, is the finest and best that we have, but I am sorry to say I hav'nt it, and never read it, but have merely seen marked allusion to it. Bishop Taché, in his work already cited on some other point, thus refers to it. " This delightful " little stream, rising to the east of Methy Portage, has, up to the pre- " sent time, and in spite of the difficulties of navigation, enjoyed almost " the exclusive privilege of supplying a route to Athabasca-McKenzie. " On descending from the heights of Methy Portage, one takes boat on "this little river, which, in order to keep the traveller in the midst of the " beauties it presents to his view, places obstructions in the way, neces- " sitating the *portages* of White Mud, the Pines, Big Stone, the Nurse " and the Cascades. The river is not navigable by other boats than " those of the country, and even then, the navigation is not easy." I copy *verbatim* from the admirable translation by Captain Cameron, R.A., of the Bishop's masterly sketch.

Mr. Simpson's account of this interesting spot is also worthy of reference. And first, as to his approach to it from *Lac de l' Ile à la Crosse.* " Early in the afternoon " [This was on the third day of his winter march from the post of *Lac de l' Ile à la Crosse,* and which post, Bishop Taché

says, (if I remember aright) is 120 miles from Methy Portage or River;
a statement which is confirmed by Simpson's itinerary.]   " We reached—
says Simpson's narrative, " Methye Lake, near the middle of which, on
" a long projecting point, we emcamped among firs of great size."
*   *   *   " After I had ascertained the latitude, 56° 28' 48 5 N. we
" quitted our snug quarters at three a.m. of the 24th."   I make the citation as marking, very reliably evidently, the precise latitude of this
" Long Point," with its " Firs."   " Scarcely had we started when the
" weather became overcast and snowy ; but we took our course by com-
" pass, across the remaining section of the lake, to the celebrated portage
" la Loche.   The snow was very deep throughout this formidable barrier,
" and the white hares, which had been strangers to us since leaving Lac
" la Crosse, now often leaped across our path."   From the hills on the
north side, a thousand feet in height, we obtained that noble view of the
" Clear Water River, which has been drawn with so much truth and beauty
" by Sir George Back ; though the dark day, and the livery of winter,
" were unfavourable to our full enjoyment of the prospect.   Launching
" down the steep and slippery descents, we turned off to the left, and
" halted for breakfast on the bank of a streamlet flowing into Clear
" Water River, distant fourteen miles from the creek which the boats
" enter at the end of this long carrying place."   *   *   " One of the
" pines, under shelter of which we took up our night's lodgings, mea-
" sured three yards in girth, at five feet from the ground,"

   " This is a fine country for the chase, and so little frequented in
" winter, that it may be regarded as an extensive preserve.   We saw
" three moose deer on the top of one of the hills ; and their tracks, and
" those of the wood-buffalo, were numerous in every direction.   The
" valley of the river is entirely sheltered from the inclement north and
" north-west winds, but its exposure to the east usually rendered the
" snow deep and soft, as we found to our cost."   Next day, " Just before
" breakfasting we saw, on the northern hills, a large moose and a band
" of five wood-buffaloes sunning their fat sides—a sight sufficient to
" make the mouths of pemican eaters water ; but they were beyond
" our reach, and taking the alarm, quickly disappeared.   The declivities
" of the hills seemed, as we passed along, completely chequered with the
" tracks of these and smaller animals."

   Such being the winter view, what must the summer one have been !
I have read, somewhere, but where I cannot tell—a description of the
" matchless scene," in its summer garb.   A valley deep, and wide anon—
a velvet lawn, three miles wide, stretching westward thirty miles or

more, in one view, with lofty sheltering hills on either side, clad to their top, with trees of varied northern kind—a beauteous sylvan blazonry— while in the vale below, viewed from its lofty source, first dashes forth this Brook of the north, plunging from rock to rock, then hurrying down " with many a silvery waterbreak" or " slipping between the ridges," till at length, with many a curve and graceful " wind about," with water crystally clear, and glittering in golden western ray, it gladdens all the vale— flowing on " to join the brimming river," and thence to the far, far, shining, thirsting sea.

In the neighborhood of this *summit source*, is another, of marked feature, viz., Lake Wollaston, large, full of islands, with a shore line of probably about three hundred miles, and from which (a great flat) flows water into two different river systems, viz., that of McKenzie's River (Arctic), and that of Churchill River (Atlantic).

NOTE XXXV.

"*Big Athabasca River.*" In contradistinction to the "Little Athabasca," (Clear Water River) just referred to, in the preceding note. The " Big Athabasca," or Athabasca River proper, draws from the glaciers of Mount Brown, the highest Peak (16,600 feet) of the Rocky Mountains, and also from a much lower height called the *Miette*, not far from the Leather or Yellow Head Pass. I have seen, but remember not the glaciers that feed this noble river, having passed and repassed them in very early life and once with " thirty feet " of snow after mid April, under foot in the pass (Athabasca Pass), the highway, then, of the Hudson's Bay Company, to the Columbia. The summit water of the Pass is common, to two oceans, the Pacific (by the Columbia River), and the Artic, by the Athabaska and McKenzie River, and which in fact, are one, the Athabasca being, though probably not the longest, yet probably the fullest tributary to the main trunk known as the McKenzie ; and which, by the geographers, (in doubt probably as to whether the Peace River, or the Athabasca was entitled to be the " Main ") has been shortened off at Lake Athabasca.

Whether quantity, or length constitute the " trunk " of a river is a thing I have not yet learned, and so far as I know is still quite a question, *e. g.*, the Nile, and the Niger.

The extended length of the great Athabasca is put at a little *under* a thousand miles, and of Peace River with its Finlay Branch, at a little over that.

Note XXXVI.

" *Only quadruped we have seen.*" And yet according to Simpson, and that in winter, the valley was full of animal life, *i.e.*, all kinds known to the region—from rabbits to wood-buffaloes. At this particular part, where the " cat was shot", Mr. Simpson speaks of the Lynxes being remarkably abundant, revelling in hare, in their favorite haunts there.

The fact is, that the noise of travellers, especially in large parties, drives off all *feræ*, into covert, except a bear now and then, when too busy at work, a-berrying or fishing about along shore for grub; but even bruin (not the " grizzly ") is very apt to scuttle off at first sight (not sound perhaps) of a stranger.

Note XXXVII.

"*Passed the Bituminous Springs.*" These Northern bituminous springs are reported on from an area of over a hundred thousand square miles between the primary rocks of the Laurentian system, and the foot of the Rocky Mountains and even some distance up their slope. Whatever be the quality or special property of this surcharge of our teeming earth in this area, it is observed by all travellers that it does no harm to any thing, not even to the trees at whose roots it comes oozing out in all its apparent nastiness. Sir John Richardson (says Mr. Russell in his authoritative work on our North West), reports that " it seems rather to increase than impair the fertility of the soil." " Striking oil " would seem to be rather an easy process in such grounds. It would be worth trying.

Note XXXVIII.

"*Large Strata of Pit Coal.*" This, no doubt, is the seam of coal "eight feet in thickness" which, at this place, Dr. Hector speaks of. It is not " pit coal," in the ordinary sense, not, at least, in quality, but in appearance. Its quality, and economic value is not yet determined, but there is no doubt that it burns well, although, it is said, it leaves much ash. On the Athabasca, and McLeod Rivers, nearer the Mountain where the rivers have worn themselves deeper channels in their soft bed of earth, gravel, mud, and sandstone, to the limestone, strata fifteen feet are exhibited in the river bank. At Fort Edmonton, I understand that it has been used, and probably still is, for blacksmith work. On the whole, I consider our coal measures of immense value, and I say so, not from my own observation, but from the gathered observations of those, who well knew coal in its varied application in their home-country (Britain), and

who had tried the thing, and found it, as Mr. McDonald stamps it,
" good as pit coal," *i. e.*., pit coal of Scotland, say of Mid Lothian, where
there are kinds, such as the " Diamond," unsurpassed in the world for
excellence and general utility.   If it was that or some other good Scotch
coal, that was in Mr. McDonald's mind, when he applied the term, it
certainly must be valuable, or, at least, have appeared so to him.   This
subject of coal in our North West is of such importance to us, that I
feel tempted to gather, and give in as succint and clear a form as the
subject will admit of, a number of the reports we have on it, from the
Saskatchewan to near the Artic Sea Coast, and westward to Vancouver's
and " Queen Charlotte Island," or Islands, from which latter place it
has been taken, in considerable quantity of late—so I have read in the
newspapers, and I think the account probably true—and that the quality
(a superior kind of anthracite, I understood, but hesitate to accept the
statement as to kind) was so good as to command a very high (almost
incredibly high) price, viz. $20 (twenty dollars) per ton, in San Fran-
cisco, where, the Vancouver coal (Nanaimo, not anthracite) was ruling at
only " $12.50 the ton," or about that ; the best *English* coal fetching
there, then, $20 the ton.   For the present however,—leaving the subject
to others to deal with—it will suffice perhaps to give an extract from
Mr. Fleming's (Sandford Fleming's) invaluable compendium as to our
North West resources, under head " Memorial of the People of Red
River to the British and Canadian Governments, with remarks on the
Colonization of British North America, and the establishment of a Great
Territorial Road from Canada to British Columbia,"—published in 1863.
Page 21.—" Geology and Mineral Wealth of the Territory."   " From
" the shores of Lake Superior to the eastern banks of Lake Winnipeg,
" the geological formation is that of the crystalline rocks, a system which
" is not generally favorable to agriculture, although here and there, many
" fertile spots are to be found.   This comparatively sterile region extends
" northward to the Arctic Sea ; Lake Athabaska, and Great Slave Lake
" being situated on its most westerly limit."

So much in introduction.   " To the westward of these lakes and
" Winnipeg,"—he goes on to say—" and between them nearly to the
" Rocky Mountains, the whole territory is of the silurian and devonian
" formations, both eminently favorable to agriculture, the former prevail-
" ing throughout the fertile peninsula of Upper Canada.   At its base,
" the silurian deposits range a thousand miles from east to west, and ex-
" tend about five hundred miles to the northward, where the devonian
" system commences and continues to the Arctic Sea.   It is part of the

" territory through which the Saskatchewan and McKenzie rivers flow,
" which is highly praised for its fertility of the prairie lands.   About one
" hundred and fifty miles east of the Rocky Mountains, the *Great Coal*
" *Bed* commences, which gives our territory so important an advantage
" over that which lies to the south.   So far as has been ascertained, it is
" over fifty miles in width."   [Note by Ed.—On the Athabasca, McLeod
and Pembina rivers, in the line of travel between Edmonton and Jasper's
House, it is found in seams from " fifteen to twenty feet in thickness "
—that was at a point fully three hundred and fifty miles, in air line,
West, or rather S.W. of " Coal Island," at the mouth of the Athabasca,
and about a hundred miles less from the bituminous spring of Mr. Mc-
Donald and Dr. Hector, just referred to. The same breadth, say 350 miles
W.N.W. is indicated by most abundant " show " on the Peace river in its
upper reaches, " and extends," proceeds Mr. Fleming, " continuously
over sixteen degrees of latitude to the Arctic Ocean."   [Four hundred
thousand square miles of coal area ! Not in one bed, however, but in
separate ones, as referred to by Mr. Fleming.]

" The lignite (or tertiary coal) formation is still more extensively de-
" veloped ; and as the occurrence of coal in these high latitudes is a
" question of much interest, the result of Sir John Richardson's obser-
" vations and enquiries on the subject, to which he has given much
" attention, are here briefly stated.

" At the junction of McKenzie and Bear Lake River, the formation
" is best exposed ; it there consists of a series of beds, the thickest of
" which exceed three yards, separated by layers of gravel and sand, alter-
" nating with a fine grained friable sandstone, and sometimes with thick
" beds of clay, the interposing layer being often dark, from the dissemin-
" ation of bituminous matter.   The coal, when recently extracted from
" the bed, is massive, and most generally shows the woody structure dis-
" tinctly.   Different beds, and even different parts of the same bed, when
" when traced to the distance of a few hundred yards, present examples
" of ' fibrous brown coal,' ' earth coal,' ' conchoidal brown coal,' and
" ' trapezoidal brown coal.'   Some beds have the external character of a
" compact bitumen, but they generally exhibit on the cross fracture con-
" centric layers, although from their jet like composition, the nature of
" the woody fibres cannot be detected by the microscope.   Some pieces
" have a strong resemblance to charcoal in structure, color and lustre.
" From the readiness with which the coal takes fire spontaneously, the
" beds are destroyed as they become exposed to the atmosphere, and
" the bank is constantly crumbling down, so that it is only when

" the debris has been washed away by the river that good sections are
" exposed."

The Simpson Narrative also speaks of the burning coal on the banks
of the McKenzie, at Bear River. "Formations similar to that found on
" McKenzie River," continues Mr. Fleming, " extend southward along
" the eastern base of the Rocky Mountains, as far as the Saskat-
" chewan River. Sir John Richardson gives a detailed account of the
" various localities between these two points in which beds of coal have
" been exposed, all pointing to the existence of a vast coal field, skirting
" the base of the Rocky Mountains for a very great extent, and con-
" tinued probably far into the Arctic Sea, where, as is well known, lignite
" apparently of a similar character has recently been discovered by Capt.
" McClure, in the same general line with the localities above mentioned."

As to our Pacific Coal Measures, I have only this to remark, before
closing this note, that by a wonderful fitness of things to an end—how
often in this word of Providence we find it so !—we have, at the " har-
bor mouth," at every natural port on our Pacific coast, viz. : Esquimault,
Burrard's Inlet, Bentinck Arm, and Observatory Inlet, inexhaustible
coal, of the best kind, all ready to tumble into the ship's hold.   I refer
more particularly, to the coal of Vancouver's and Queen Charlotte Islands.

NOTE XXXIX.

" *Athabasca Lake*," or " Lake of the Hills."—The " hills " are where
the great Laurentian primary, like a wall, bounds the base of that vast
Silurian slope—that ancient sea-bottom of limestone—which, without a
break, and gently, almost imperceptibly gradual, extends far up the
eastern side of the Rocky Mountains, and at the " Passes," " Yellow
Head," and " Peace River," extends to the very summit of the height of
land between Atlantic and Arctic watershed on the one hand, and
Pacific on the other hand.

This picturesque and beautiful sheet of cold, clear, snow-fed crystal
water is about two hundred miles, but probably scarcely that, in length,
from east to west, and is about forty-five in width at the broadest part.

The *level* of the Lake above sea has not, so far as I know, been made
an object of special observation by any of the men of science who have
passed that way, with the exception, most probably, of Colonel Lefroy.

In the present juncture of " Question of Rocky Mountain Passes," it
would have been of some advantage to have had a well determined
starting point for measurement of Pacific passes in those latitudes, say
such a point as the west end of the Lake, or mouth of Peace River.   But

I must, at the same time, admit that I have not read the reports of Colonel Lefroy, or of other officers acting under the Imperial authorities in survey of late years of the North West Territories, but merely a few of their statements, here and there, indirectly, as given by others.   In the hurry, *currente calamo*, of this writing (for it has been suddenly called forth only within the last few days, and the work can be done only at moments stolen from pressing professional avocations, and altogether is only about a ten days' " round of work " of a hundred hours or so.)   I am forced, with much regret, to draw my conclusions—unavoidably crude in many instances—merely from that accidental personal knowledge, and special garnered literature, viz., journals, reports, letters, &c., of relatives and friends in the Hudson's Bay Company's service, throughout their whole vast field of operations, which accident has thrown in my way, and which I happen to command.   With this special knowledge, and also that general knowledge which is to be gathered from even the " popular books " of the day, and, let me add, a good deal of blue book, I make bold, in the present discussion of Pacific Routes, to advance an opinion.   I did it before, under the *nom de plume* " Britannicus," in the Ottawa *Times*, during Dominion Session, 1869, before the issue of Mr. Rnssell's or Mr. Waddington's pamphlet (which latter I have not yet seen), and the acknowledgment, by the Press, of the " public service," on that occasion, has, it would seem, given food to vanity.   But to proceed—

The only statement that I have come across as to " level " is in Bishop Taché's sketch (page 33), where he says : " It is a beautiful expanse of " limpid water, measuring over 200 miles in length, at an elevation of " about 600 feet above sea-level."

" About 600 feet " is, I think, a correct estimate—rather over, perhaps, but, for present argument, fairly predicable.

Unfortunately, however, the " Sketch " excusably perhaps as a mere sketch, does not give authorities for the statement.   Perhaps there were none.   I assume, for the nonce, that there are none, and that we have to make it out as best we can.   It is worth trying.

Firstly.   We have evidence from abundant scientific report that, from the mouth of McKenzie to that of the Mississippi, and also to that of the St. Lawrence, there once—just before our era—rolled and flowed a mighty glacial sea, whose traces, surface traces, (viz., sea-shells, of present congeners on the Greenland coast, and ice grooves, and ice-borne boulder deposits, all the way from Quebec to Norway House, and thence to the shore of the Arctic Ocean) are to found at a uniform height of about 650

feet above our present sea level. That between us and the North Pole
(or rather between the nearest dry land down here, and the Pole, for
Ottawa was then at " the bottom of the deep blue sea ") there was nought
of " land," save where the old Laurentian reared, in long iron-bound
coast, broken and fiorded like that of Norway, Greenland and British
Columbia, its rugged face of rock. From the outlet of Great Bear Lake,
thence to the hills of Lake Athabasca (its northern and eastern
bordering), thence to Lake Winnipeg (also its northern and eastern
bordering), thence along the north of Lakes Superior and Huron, and
thence to our ancient sea beaches (plain, bare and smooth as when
washed by the billow) on the Rigaud Mountain and other corresponding
heights, on the neighbouring Laurentian Range, we can, with marked
distinctness trace an ancient shore line ; and at the foot of that
shore, the *remnant pools*—very large, if you will, but still, comparatively, *pools*—of that great ocean subsidence, which gave us the
Mountain of Montreal, with its Greenland sea shells at its top, *just*
about " 650 feet above the level of the sea." In this " 650 feet level "
we find a remarkable identity in all these great lakes. Superior, Huron,
Michigan, and I might add Erie, are all well determined as to almost
identity of level. So is Winnipeg (630 feet). Now, from the Winipeg
level to Cumberland House, the rise on the Saskatchewan, as given by
Professor Hihd, on careful " levelling," as he says, is as follows:—
" Grand Rapids" forty-three and-a-half feet, viz., the lower part fifteen
feet, and the upper part 28·58 feet (see page 78 of his Report, 1859,
giving the report of Mr. John Fleming.) From the head of the rapid to
Cumberland House (which, though not actually on the Saskatchewan, is
only two miles from it, and on the same level there), the Saskatchewan,
as reported by Professor Hind, and as shown by Mr. McDonald's
Journal, and as shown, in fact, by every account we have of the route,
is, to the extent of nearly one-third, lacustrine, and the rest of very little
current. The distance from the head of the rapid is given at about 175
miles.

About eight inches to the mile would, I consider, be a liberal allowance for fall to that point. From that point to the lake add, the " forty-
three and-a-half feet," and we have about 160 feet as the height at
Cumberland House above Winnipeg Lake, of the water route we are
following.

From Methy Portage to Frog Portage there are, according to Bishop
Taché (*expertem credite*, for he has travelled the route, and that, with a
very closely observing intelligence, as appears from his report), " 300 to

400 miles of Churchill River Waters, but only navigable with the canoes in use."

Of this distance, there is, he says, "about 120 miles in which there is no obstruction to navigation, namely, from the southern extremity of *L'Ile à la Crosse* Lake to the mouth of Methy River," (near the end, if not at the end of the portage). The bad part, is bad indeed, according to his description, full of cascades and rapids. Yet, we see those over-lasting "four or five ton boats" of the Company regularly ascend them and descend them without material difficulty. There does not seem to be any "fall" of any height in the whole distance, but only "bad cascades and rapids." Allowing for the 120 miles "so good," say 100 feet, and for the rest 250, we have 450 feet from this end of Methy Portage to the head of Frog Portage. Frog Portage is, as stated in the map, only 370 yards, and is, according to all accounts, level, in fact, at high water in Spring, the waters flow over. From it to Cumberland House is about 200 miles, much of it lake, and the rest of easy river navigation. The Journal shows this—allow 200 feet of fall (*pente*) for that. The total from Methy Portage to Cumberland House we then have at 650 ; which being added to the 160 of Cumberland height above Winipeg gives us a grand total of 810, from Winipeg Lake to the lower end of Methy Portage add ninety feet (a liberal estimate), for rise of portage to its culmination at the "Laurentide" brink, overlooking the "Clear Water," and we have 900 feet as the height of that height above the Winipeg level. The Winipeg level, as that of Lakes Superior, Huron and Michigan, so well known and indisputable—is about 630 feet above the sea—we have, therefore, at this point, say Methy Portage, a height of 1,530 feet above the level of the sea. Simpson, who is ever scrupulously, and I may say, scientifically correct, calls the "towering height " "*above*" him, only " 1,400 " feet, and, of course, in the fervour of the moment, he naturally gave the "highest possible estimate." Perhaps he meant 1,400 above the immediate level beneath; but it matters not. To the valley beneath is, by all, called a descent great and sudden, but none, even to round a period, exceed the traditional "1,000 feet." Let us, in all fairness again, call it 800, from the 1,530 aforesaid, and we have 730 remainder, *i.e.*, to the river at our feet. But there are still about 200 miles of river to descend, and for which nine inches a mile of descent would be but fair allowance, say 150 feet, leaving, therefore, for height of level of the Lake (Athabasca) *only* 580 feet (*five hundred and eighty feet*) above the sea.

But, secondly, to measure it from another direction.

From Lake Athabasca—say Fort Chipewyan, the point whence issues the McKenzie—to the Arctic Ocean is a course of very slow river flow, and much of it, lake, without a single " fall," and with only four rapids—and they not of any markedly great descent, nor long, viz., the " Cassette," " Mountain," " Pelican," and that of " The Drowned," all between Arthabasca and Great Slave Lake.   The distance by the river may be a thousand miles, say twelve hundred, the ordinary voyages, by those fair measures of travel, the ever present " four or five ton boat " of the North, and also the recorded time and incidents of the expeditionary passages over that old highway to the Arctic, indicating that as a fair predicate of length.   In air-line it is about 700 statute miles, as established by well-determined points, viz., Fort Chipewyan, latitude 58°. 42'. 38". N., Longitude 111° 18' 22" W., according to Simpson, who seems to have made his observations with great care, and is in perfect accord—so I would gather from his narrative—with Sir John Franklin ;—the other point being " Shingle Point," at the mouth of the McKenzie, precisely on the " 69° " parallel of north latitude.   The Longitude is not given, but according to map, is about 136° W.   The Simpson expedition was thirty-nine days (from 1st June to 9th July) on the route between these points, but was detained twelve days by ice on Great Slave Lake, and four or five days by stoppages at posts, making arrangements for winter quarters on Great Bear Lake, and by adverse winds too strong for their boats, though descending the river.   I give these details, as elements for estimate.   The estimate I make, is an average of six inches of river fall per mile from Lake Athabasca to the Ocean, say 1,200 miles, which gives us just 600 feet for level height of that sheet.

Thirdly ; The only other stated height in this region, and it is one of which there might be less doubt than as to the true meaning of Simpson's 1,400 feet, is that of the old and ever important post, known as " Fort Liard," in latitude 59° 40' N., or about that, and longitude 121° 40' W., or about that, in a direction west, or almost due west from the northern side of the lake, and about 300 miles *nearer* the Rocky Mountains, from which, according to Russell (page 35), it is distant only " fifty miles." According to the same authority—and we cannot have higher than Mr. Russell, because he speaks ever from authentic record—the height of that spot is only " 400 or 500 feet above the sea."   If it be so, then Lake Athabasca must be considerably less, if there be—as we know there is—slope eastwards from the Rocky Mountains. There are also geologic and geographic facts of particular bearing on the point, which I might adduce in the argument, but I have said enough I think. No one can reasonably object to "600," at least, as a "bench mark" here, for our clime over the Rocky Mountains, *via* Peace River.

Note XL.

" *Fort Chipewyan* " (pronounced Tchippiwyan), is, according to Simpson's itinerary, " 371 miles from *Ile à la Crosse*." It was, in the times of the old North-West Company's sway in that region, a very important post, an " emporium," as Mr. McDonald truly reports of it. But " times had changed " with it, evidently. Simpson, preparing for his expedition, building boats, &c., spent all February, March, April and May there. " May," says he, " like April, was a fine month; but, till near its close, " there was little sultry weather." Swallows appeared about the houses on the 19th, and, during the whole month the geese (four kinds he names, viz., the Snow, Canada, Laughing and Hutchin's–the first, most numerous) " on their northward migration, afforded the Camp food, and the fort " sportsmen amusement." * * * " On the 11th we had smart thunder- " storms." " Owing to the general (meaning *unusual*, I presume*)* " coolness of the season, and the low state of the waters, the ice lingered " on the lake until the 22nd." " All attempts to raise produce among " rocks at Fort Chipewyan have proved abortive, even potatoes being " brought down from Peace River." " On the 23rd, the Peace River " boats reached English Island, and their cargoes were carried by land to " the establishment, a distance of two miles." On account of the lake- ice, of course. These little entries tell their own tale, and they are notes worth noting on the way.

Note XLI.

" *Just a month since we left York Factory.* "

Considering the character of the route, forty miles a day, stoppages included, would be a fair average. This would give about 1,200 miles as the distance of Fort Chipewyan from York Factory, *via* Methy Portage.

Note XLII.

" *The Governor closed his public correspondence.* "

Governor Simpson had a remarkable administrative ability, to which he bent an industry which did the work of two or three other ordinary men. I see in the "Cassette " full of these old Hudson's Bay papers now before me, that his " private " correspondence with the " gentlemen " in the trade, as the phrase used to be, was no inconsiderable work. He, at one

time, so overtaxed himself in that way, as to become partially blind, and
in 1840, when in London, used to make me his reader to him of an
evening. Most kindly, he tried to get me to enter the service, but this
animal would not.

Note XLIII.

Chief Factor's Commission to Mr. Peter Warren Dease.—Mr. Dease
was at the head of the Franklin Expedition of 1825-6-7, in conducting
it in all its working, details, commissariat, &c., leaving the higher work
of taking observations and making notes by the way, free and untram-
meled, to Sir John Franklin. He did his work well; and according to
what has ever been a rule with the company in such case, Mr. Dease was
at once promoted from his Chief Tradership to a Chief Factorship, which
is a " double share," and entails no extrawork. A good thing, for those
who could get it.

It was for like service on the subsequent expedition (that of "Dease
and Sinpson,") of 1837-8-9, which completed the survey of our north
coast from Franklin's furthest, west of the McKenzie, and also for much
new discovery on the east side, and north of the Coppermine River,
that knighthood, we have already alluded to, was offered to Mr. Dease.
On his refusal of the honor, the Imperial Government offered him a pen-
sion of a hundred pounds sterling. On his retirement in 1841-2, he
settled in the immediate neighborhood of Montreal, where even among
the other old tall Nor-Westers that used then to walk the streets of their
old emporium, Mr. Dease, tall, straight and strong, and of noble mien,
towered above the rest. He was of a class, great and grand, in many
respects, but they are gone, as warriors, of old, and we this younger gen-
eration at least, are reaping the fruits of their conquest. The story is too
long for this note.

Note XLIV.

Cariboo Mountain at a distance to our right.—I don't know where to
find a description of this range of hills, for the word " mountain " is a
very indefinite term, and conveys no more measure of height or size than
a " piece of chalk." In Arrowsmith's, which, as I have said before, is to
be thoroughly relied on, at least the one before me, one made expressly for
the Company, or, at least, on the face of it, dedicated, by permission, to them,
and " containing " as stated on the face of it, " the best information
" which the Company's documents, (placed at his command), furnished."
In this most reliable map, I find a very well marked and regular range

of hills laid down from near where the Peace River " forks," at the pass
in the Mountains, to the McKenzie River at Mountain Portage, about 120
miles by river course, say 100 miles in air-line, nearly due north of Fort
Chipewyan.   The range runs at an average distance of from thirty to fifty
miles from this part of the river, where occurs the most northerly bend in
it, and is as a wall stretching from the Rocky Mountains to the Laurentian rock, on the eastern side of the McKenzie, at Mountain Portage.
Be the hills or " mountains " high or low, they undoubtedly have a most
beneficial effect in sheltering the " happy valley " from rude Boreas.   I
say valley, for on reference to the map, and also to other accounts of the
topography of that region, I find that from this very point spoken of in
the Journal, there is another a range of hills, the " Deer Mountains," low in
the lower part of the slope between the Rocky Mts and Athabasca Lake,
but gradually increasing in height, until at Lesser Slave Lake, (the north-
west end of which, the range seems to overlap), it attains a height of "800
ft." or about that above the Lake.   From that north-west end to the Yellow
Head Pass, the ridge, " low swelling"—for that is what it seems to fall off
to—is distinct enough to form the established boundary in that direction,
between the Lesser Slave District and that of Peace River, as laid out
by the Company for their work.   The Peace River trading district extends from this boundary, which terminates at the Yellow Head Pass, to a
point about 500 miles north along the ridge of the Rocky Mountains,
thence eastward about 200 miles towards the McKenzie River along a
river from the Rocky Mts. called Nahanie, and passing about 100 miles
north of Fort Liard, thence traversing the Cariboo Mts, and Peace River
about twenty miles above the Falls hereinafter mentioned, up Loon River,
or the river discharging from Loon Lake, about thirty miles below Fort
Vermilion, and thence to the Yellow Head Pass, following the height
of land, (the southern range of the valley aforesaid,) between the waters
flowing into the Peace River—such as the large Smoky River and its
tributaries—and the waters—the multitude of hill streams—that pour
into Lesser Slave Lake.

   The lower District on the Peace River is the one known as the Athabasca District.

   These are natural boundaries, and would answer well for any purpose
of territorial division.   They have been disturbed, however, by the
Imperial Act, 29 and 30 Victoria, chap. 67, defining, or rather giving in
its new constitution, boundaries to British Columbia.   By that Act, the
eastern boundary is laid down thus :—" And to the East, from the
boundary of the United States, northwards by the Rocky Mountains,

and the one hundred and twentieth meridian of West Longitude." This Meridian is five degrees east of the Rocky Mountains at the northern boundary of this District, and bisects it transversely. Why the old boundary, viz. : the Rocky Mountains, was not retained, I cannot conceive, unless (as would almost seem to be the case) our Imperial Legislators assumed that the Rocky Mountains and the 120° West Longitude were identical, or nearly so. They are not, but vary fully *fifteen degrees* at the northern boundary (Arctic Shore) of British Columbia ; the result of which is, that the lower three or four hundred miles of McKenzie's River now belong to British Columbia. For once, at least, the Hudson's Bay Company seem to have been asleep when they allowed, without protest, such interference with their possessory rights. The new boundary gives British Columbia the Peace River Pass and nearly one hundred miles east of it.

I give the boundaries of this most interesting District with some particularity, because they have been originally laid down with that, I may say, consummate wisdom which marks, or marked at the time in question, those old merchant adventurers of the North—the North-West Company and the Hudson's Bay Company. The North-West were undoubtedly the first on this field, and to their memory is due the *"pas"* of precedence. These boundaries as a principle, were geographical, and adopted with the view of most easy concentration for local trade, and in subservience, in some measure, to tribal habitats.

There is also this specialty to call for remark in this direction. The Upper Peace River district, and immediately beyond, on the Pacific, is even already known and worked as a gold region, and even already government, with its assigned local limits, and local administrations may be necessary. The people pouring in there from the comparatively exhausted gold fields of California and Cariboo, are entitled to that protection of law and order, which I fear is not to be found there at present. The first difficulty to cope with,—and it is a most formidable one,—in those parts of British Columbia, is the Indian one. The Indian must be bought or killed, else *he* will kill. I make the remark here, although it may not be strictly in place, nor fitting for the work more immediately in hand.

Note XLV.

" Northern Lights." The familiar sight requires no explanation. As to the mooted point, however, of *audibleness,* I find a strange diversity of opinion, of experience rather, as reported by friends of the far North.

I have seen these lights myself in our " higher latitudes," and, of course, wondered with open eye and ear at the phenomenon,—the dance of " The mystic North Men." To me—though of good ear—it was ever silent. On the other hand there are some—credible thoroughly—who, conscientiously, declare that they have heard the sound, as of the rustling of silk. Electric, it may, possibly, have made small *thunder*, to their finer sense, or imagination.

Note XLVI.

" *Grand Falls*," *ten or fifteen feet high*." These are the only " Falls" in the whole course of the river from beyond the *other* side of the Rocky Mountains, and the only place throughout the whole of it, at which, a canoe had to be taken out of the water, in so far as appears from Mr. McDonald's narrative, or any account of the route that I ever came across, or read, or heard allusion to. These " Falls" are about 220 miles from the mouth of Peace River.

Note XLVII.

" *Fort Vermilion*." About 320 miles from the mouth of Peace River is, or at least used to be, a post of considerable importance in the trade, but not the chief post, Dunvegan, higher up, being the *Chef-lieu* of the district. " Mr. Paul Fraser," a clerk in the service, was then in charge, as appears from Mr. McDonald's journal. Amongst my father's old papers, I find one, on some point of business, from this same Paul Fraser, dated 1st May, 1827, the year before the present voyage, addressed to my father as officer in charge at Norway House. I refer to it merely to show that the *mail* boat, or canoe, or in other words the craft with the precious " returns " for the whole district, which must have started from Dunvegan (250 miles up stream) four or five days or more before, passed here as early as 1st May, when, of course, the river must have been perfectly clear of ice.

Note XLVIII.

" *Found the two with a moose*." Killed just at the spot, the distant camping place, where wanted. All the accounts of the abundance of Moose, (Elk, as Sir Alexander McKenzie calls them,) different kinds of deer, and wood buffalo, throw " Gordon Cumming's Africa," into shade. Hear Sir Alexander on the theme ! Speaking from a spot about eighty miles above where Fort Vermilion now is, but on the south or west side of the river, he says, under date 1793, 10th May :—" At this time, the

" buffaloes were attended with their young ones that were frisking
" around them ; and it appeared that the elks would soon exhibit the
" same enlivening circumstance.   The whole country displayed an exhu-
" berant verdure ; the trees that bear a blossom were advancing fast to
" that delightful appearance, and the velvet rind of their branches
" reflecting the oblique rays of a rising or setting sun, added a splendid
" gaiety to the scene which no expressions of mine are qualified to des-
" cribe."

And further on, from a spot on the same side, at a bend of the river
where the first " McLeod's Fort," of Peace River was built, about fifty
miles below Dunvegan, the illustrious traveller discourseth thus, about
the same date of course :—

" Here the ground rises at intervals to a considerable height, and
"stretching inwards " (*i.e.,* towards the south-east, in the direction of
Lesser Slave Lake and the Athabasca River) " at every interval or
" pause in the rise there is a very gently ascending space or lawn with
" abrupt precipices, to the summit of the whole, or at least as far as the
" eye could distinguish.   This magnificent theatre of nature has all the
" decorations which the trees and animals of the country can afford it ;
" groves of poplars in every shape vary the scene, and their intervals
" are enlivened with vast herds of elks and buffaloes, the former choosing
"the steeps and uplands, and the latter preferring the plains."   See
Journal, p. 155.

Another scene is described as being like a " cattle yard."

Further on in his journal, Mr. McDonald speaks of thirteen bags of
pemican, besides four bales of ditto or meat being made out of one day's
slaughter of the animals about the Fort, *i.e.,* moose, buffaloes, &c. ; each
bag and bale weighs 90 lbs, and it may be imagined what killing there
must have been.   Mr. McDonald, like Sir Alexander McKenzie, was a
fur trader, and wisely prosecuted his calling for his own concern, and not,
by his "travellers' tales" over true, to bring interlopers into the country
to spoil the business.

Note XLIX.

" *Large columns of black earth.*"   Oozing out of the sandstone, no
doubt a bituminous mixture of some economic value, if intelligently
applied—but how, or for what purpose, save as a sort of paint, or boat,
or roof, or wood pitching for preservation, I cannot say.   There is this,
however, to be said of it, that possibly it might be available for making
into *briquette,* an artificial fuel of coal-dust and something else, pressed,

and dried, and now used largely in the Austrian, Belgian, and French railways. A similar compound has lately been submitted by one Loyseau to the Franklin Institute, in Philadelphia. The briquette has been found to evaporate seven times its weight of water, and has been found to be the cheapest of fuel for railways, in Europe.

This "black earth" is most probably highly bituminous. In any case it is worth testing. The phenomenon *here* is interesting, as showing the extent of this bituminous area, or area of bitumen, the other exhibit of it, last alluded to, being that at or near the mouth of the Pembina on the Athabasca, fully three hundred miles in western air line from this spot.

Note L.

"*Smoky River.*"—A large tributary, with itself many tributaries carrying the waters of the large area between Peace River, and the Deer Mountains ; running from the west end of Lesser Slave Lake, and the Yellow Head Pass. The distance from Dunvegan, or mouth of Smoky River, to the Yellow Head Pass, S.W., and following the general course of that stream, is, in air line,—and the route by road would not be ten per cent more,—about 150 miles, but the difference in level, or height above sea, I estimate at about 2,000 feet:—Of this more anon. I mention these distances and features, in view of a territorial grand trunk road, with branches, in this direction.

Note LI.

"*Delightful country that we have passed through to day.*"—It was, or rather would have been, "delightful" throughout, all along, had the the travellers been on the high bank of the river, instead of in the bottom of its trough, very deep trough. Here, where they stopped for dinner, viz., at an "Old house of Mr. David Thompson," and where the "Freeman," Bastonais was living *en Seigneur*, they were in the open, and could then, as Sir Alexander McKenzie, at the same spot did, get a view of the *delightful* country all around.

Note LII.

"*Poires,*" or "*Sascutum berries.*"—"Saskerum," is the word in the M.S., but, to my ear and memory, it should be Sass-kootum, with the accent on the first syallable. The "Poire," so called from its elongated oval shape, somewhat like a pear save in having no *smaller* end It is, when in full growth, fully half an inch in length, and half that in diameter, and is small seeded ; in fact, a North American raisin, luscious, wholesome, and much used as an article of food. It is put in the finer preparations of Pemican. Such Pemican is *sans pareil* as a "preserved meat."

It is said that wherever these *poires* grow, *wheat* will grow, and grow well. The alluvial flats at and towards the mouth of Peace River, from the Falls to the Lake, and rich gravelly loams above, up as far as Dunvegan, or at least up to the plains thereabout, I look upon as good wheatfield, in fact, superior wheat ground. In this connection it is worthy of note, that at the Paris Exhibition of 1867, it was a far *Northern wheat*, viz., that of John Meldrum, of Pontiac, the extreme North Western County of the Province of Qnebec, that took the second prize for wheat. Mr. Meldrum (an intelligent Scotch farmer aud miller) described to me the soil on which he grew it, and it corresponds with that which, I take it, is to be found in the Peace River Country, over the most of its extent— It was a Scotch, or more particularly, a Fifeshire wheat, that Mr. Meldrum, got the award for—The award was actually made to *him* for this wheat, but by mistake he got the diploma for " cereals," which Sir William Logan, an exhibitor of " cereals," (a collection), should have got, according to award, and Sir William got the one for the " wheat," which Mr. Meldrum, was entitled to.—Mr. Meldrum did not exhibit anything but wheat, and could not therefore, properly get the prize for " cereals " *i.e.* collection of cereals. I mention these particulars, to bring out an important fact, and at the same time, to meet any doubt on the subject. Pontiac, in climate, corresponds with that of the lower and middle part of Peace River. At Fort Liard, on, or very near the 60th parallel of N latitude nearly 4° N. of Dunvegan, and only about a hundred miles west of its meridian, " barley and oats yield good crops, and in favorable seasons, *wheat* ripens well." So says Sir John Richardson. (See Russell, page 18).

NOTE LIII.

Dunvegan.—Is on the most southern bend of the Peace River, say about 150 miles, in a straight line, from the ridge line of the Rocky Mountains. Its latitude is given by Thompson, at 56° 08, and by Colonel Lefroy at 56°. 06. N. The height above sea of this interesting place is a subject on which it is impossible to come to an absolute conclusion. Thompson puts it at one thousand feet, Lefroy, at nine hundred and ten feet, and Richardson at seven hundred and eighty feet ; Russell gives all this in his pages 75 and 81, and then in page 74, he says, " Colonel Lefroy gives 1,600 (one thousand six hundred) feet as the elevation of the country *about* Dunvegan above the sea." If " 1,600," be not a misprint for 1,000, and if he means not the hills or rising ground immediately back of Dunvegan, viz, the lower slopes of the Deer Mountains, I cannot reconcile the statements, and in fact, in any way, I cannot reconcile the statements. But there is another statement which still more involves the matter, he says—"The general elevation of the country, however, still continues to increase, and at Dunvegan it is six hundred feet above the bed of the stream ; yet even at this point, except in approaching the deep gorges, through which the tributaries of Peace River join its waters, there is little or no indication of an elevated country ; the Rocky Mountains are not visible, and no range of hills meets the eye." Add to this, the fact already recorded by Russell, page 35, and already alluded to in a preceeding note, that Fort Liard, about a hundred miles nearer the Rocky Mountains, only fifty miles from them, is *under* five hundred feet above the sea. This matter of altitude according to these varying statements is certainly, to me, at least, a puzzle. But its solution is not of such pressing moment as the ascertainment, so far as may be possible, of the *height of the Peace River Pass, through the Rocky Mountains :* to that I shall, hereafter, more particularly address myself, in my present writing.

On the question of climate, I give the following :

Table of mean temperatures in the North-west Territory and Canadian Provinces compared.

Months.	Dunvegan, Peace River, Alt. 1,000 ft. above the sea. Lat. 56°08' N., Long. 117°13' W. Obs. by D. Thompson, 1803.	Toronto, Alt. 340 feet above the sea. Lat. 43°40' N., Long. 79°22' West. Obs. by Professor Hind.	Quebec, Alt. 350 feet above the sea. Lat. 46°49' N., Obs. Long. not given. by Lieut. Ashe.	Halifax, N. S., Alt. 15 feet above the sea. Lat. 44°39' N., Long. 63°38'. From paper read by Colonel Byers at the Nova Scotia Institute of Science.
	Fahr. ° '	Fahr. ° '	Fahr. ° '	Fahr. ° '
April	37 6	41 2	37 9	38
May	64	51 5	51 6	48
June	64 5	61	63 1	56 3
July	63	66 3	67 5	62 3
August	60	65 7	65 9	63 7
September	55	57 4	57 6	57
October	40	45	44 6	47
Mean	54 87	55 44	53 45	53 18
Mean of three summer months	62 50	64 33	65 50	60 76
November	14 6	36 1	34 1	39 3
December	− 4	27	17 7	25 7
January	÷7	24 8	11 7	25
February	÷2	23 7	14 8	24 3
March	22 5	30 2	25 1	29
Mean	8 42	28 36	20 68	28 66
Mean of the year	35 51	44 16	40 99	42 69

As to the period of cultivation (from April to October) it is a fact worth noting, that Dunvegan, Toronto and Quebec, according to these tables, do not vary more than about half a degree in mean temperature, and that as to Halifax, the difference is 1°69—not far from two degree,—in favor of Dunvegan. As to the winter cold of Dunvegan, its steadiness and dryness are, for both man and beast, better than that of any other place in the Dominion, save Manitoba, perhaps.

At the same time Dunvegan is nearly thirteen degrees of latitude North of Toronto, and is, moreover, far inland, and high, while our Queen City of the Lakes, low sitting, on her 349 feet above sea, has, as mighty reservoirs of heat about her, Lakes Ontario, Erie and Huron, to warm her with their steamy vapours, when the frost gets very severe. Dunvegan (so called after the cold, bleak, rock built castle of the McLeods of Skye), has no such winter wrapper, save what vapours it may get from over the Mountain; vapours whose laws of action, most probably, would account for the singularity, according to the thermometrical register, of the January and February *decrease* of cold, from the four below zero of December. Possibly there may have been error in transcription of registry. In original entry, I know there could not have been; for, as I have before said or intimated, Mr. Thompson, to my personal knowledge (for I knew him intimately), was too scrupulously and habitually correct in such matter of professional duty, to make any such mistake.

Speaking on this subject of climate, at this spot, he says: "Only twice "in the month of May, 1803, on the 2nd and 14th, did the thermometer, "at 5 a.m., fall to 30°, and only twice was it as low at that hour, and "that, never after the fourteenth of that month. Frost did not occur "in the fall till the 27th September." "It freezes," says Mr. Russell, "much later in May, in Canada; and at Montreal for seven years out of "the last nine, the first frost occurred between 24th August and 16th "September."

In this statement as to Montreal, Mr. Russell does not give his authority, nor state the time, the year or years, he refers to, but that does not matter. The Montreal tables are accessible to all.

Mr. McKenzie says of the country, about a hundred miles above Dunvegan: "Some parts offer beautiful scenery, in some degree similar to "that which we passed on the *second* day of our voyage," [indicating remarkable equality throughout the Peace River valley, to the very Mountains], "and equally enlivened with elk and buffalo, which were "feeding in great numbers."

"A little further," (I am quoting from Russell), "twelve miles above

Sinew River, close to the Rocky Mountains," he says : " The land above
" where we camped spreads into an extensive plain, and stretches on to a
" high ridge, which in some parts presents a face of rock, but is principally
" covered with verdure, and varied with the poplar and white birch tree.
" The country is so crowded with animals as to have the appearance in
" some places of a stall yard, from the state of the ground, and the quan-
" tity of dung that is scattered over it. The soil is black and light."

Two days journey, by the river, above this, where the country is wooded heavily, Mr. McKenzie speaks, in crossing a portage, of the forest being of spruce and birch, and the largest poplars he had ever seen. Further on, he speaks of "travelling through *heavy woods* of spruce, red pine,
" cypress, poplar, white birch and willow, and through *tall pine woods.*
" Soil light, and of a dusty color, over gravelly clay. The river, still from
" *400 to 800 yards wide,* diminishing to 200 where confined. It is here
" *passing through the Rocky Mountains,* which do not rise apparently
" more than 1,500 feet above their base—bare of wood in the upper
" parts, wooded at the base. *The bed of the river is limestone, and the*
" *Mountains solid masses of the same.*"

On the 27th May, the trees, towards the bases, were, he says, putting
forth their leaves. Towards the Forks of the Findlay and South Branch
—which was that taken by the canoes, to McLeod's Lake, as stated in
Mr. McDonald's journal—he (McKenzie) speaks of the Mountains being
covered with wood.

Such is the *spring,* early May, picture of the interesting scene. The
fact is, as appears from the description of the canoe route as given in
Mr. McDonald's journal in approaching the Forks, and of them, and past
them, where there is not a word about current, or difficulties of any kind,
but only of "fine dry beaches," " prairies," &c. ; and also from Sir Alex.
McKenzie's description of that part of the route, where he speaks of
heavy woods, and travelling through tall pine woods, the very heart of
the Pass itself is a pine, and comparatively level woodland and prairie, in
varied form, but ever pleasing.

NOTE LIV.

" *Death of Mr. Hughes and four men at St. Johns.*"—From an attack
by Beaver Indians ("a warlike race,") in revenge for "wife lifting"
(so charged at least), on the part of the person in charge of the post at
the time, a Mr. Black, and who, I have understood from my father, was
some time after, in the country of the *Nez Percés,* of the Columbia, shot
dead, in his own room, by some unseen hand, from behind. The "murder

at St. Johns," as the occasion was called, seems, from the correspondence (now before me) from all the posts around within a radius of three hundred miles, to have created much alarm, and considerable disturbance of the trade. The " Beaver Indians," ever well fed, and a mountain race, are of a character of much force, and naturally of much spirit. Masters of the country they are, and have ever been; and their motto may have been, like those who built Dunvegan, of a reading to make the " Black Act" a dangerous one. I am not aware that the Sabine experiment—if ever really done—was ever repeated there, or any where else, in the Company's realms, after that.

NOTE LV.

" *Strong Current.*"—This is the first mention of strong current, or even " current " in the whole route from the mouth of this great river, so well, in this respect, called Peace River. I forget, at this moment, the Indian name, but I remember that the word means peace or stillness. Still, considering the slope from the pass in the Rocky Mountains to Lake Athabasca, say twelve hundred feet, or an average of about one foot six inches to the mile, (a predicate beyond, I believe, the actual fact), and the fact that there are no lakes nor lacustrine enlargements on the way, but one continuous river flow, with but one break, viz., the Falls, there must be considerable current part of the way, say from the Pass to Dunvegan. In the lower part it seems to be more like a large canal, than a river of the mountains. A Nile like current. The points made each day by the canoes indicate this. To Fort Vermillion, about 320 miles from mouth of Peace River, took them only six days, less two hours, of paddling, and a short portage at the Falls. From Fort Vermillion to Dunvegan is, according to the best calculation I can make—for accounts all differ— about 250 miles. The time taken was six days. So far, therefore, the current seems to have been a very gentle one throughout, but, of course, slightly increasing in the upper courses of the river. And the question here arises. How can that be so gentle a one, when Dunvegan is, as reported, so many feet, (1,600 according to Colonel Lefroy), above the sea. The explanation can be best given by citation from Russell, page 74 : " He says," *i.e.*, Colonel Lefroy, whom the author is referring to, " the stream is more rapid above Fort Vermillion than below it, and that the depth of the bed of the river below the surrounding country, increases with great uniformity upwards. About sixty miles above Fort Vermillion, where it has cut through alternating sandstone and limestone cliffs to a bed of shale, it flows at a depth of 200 feet below their summits. Then

giving the very words of Colonel Lefroy's report, he says, " The general
" elevation of the country, however, still continues to increase, and at
" Dunvegan it is six hundred feet above the bed of the stream." See extract
already given in Note LIII. As to the size and character of the river at
different parts, it will be found in the following extract from the same
authoritative quarter: " At low water the Peace River does not exceed
" a quarter of a mile in breadth below the falls: at the falls it is four hundred
yards." [Mr. McDonald, it will be remembered, calls it half a mile, but,
of course, he did not, like Colonel Lefroy, measure it. " Its width up to
" the Rocky Mountains continues much the same, sometimes attaining
" eight hundred yards. *It has much less descent than the Saskatchewan.*"

As to the river and its banks, below the Falls, McKenzie says :—" The
" country in general is low from the entrance of the river to the Falls,
" and with the exception of a few open parts covered with grass, it is
" clothed with wood. Where the banks are very low the soil is good,
" being composed of the sediment of the river and putrified leaves and
" vegetables. Where they are more elevated, they display a face of
" yellowish clay, mixed with small stones. On a line with the Falls, and
" on either side of the river, there are said to be very extensive plains
" which afford pasture to numerous herds of buffaloes." I give all this
to shew that the country there is low and flat, and current therefore
slow.

" From the Falls,"—this fine painter of Nature goes on to say—" the
" banks of the river are in general lofty, except at low woody points,
" accidentally formed in the manner I have mentioned : they also dis-
" played in all their broken parts a face of clay, intermixed with stones.
" In some places there likewise appeared a *black mould.*"

I give, to avoid mutilation, these extracts in full, although they contain
more than is necessary for the argument more immediately in hand.

The *Current*, therefore, so far from Fort Vermillion to the mouth of the
river, seems to be the gentlest possible for a river.

There are two or three rapids, mere currents between narrowing
banks, besides the Falls or one Fall aforesaid, but so slight that the
McDonald Journal does not speak of them.

The present point of "Strong Current" is reached early on the day
after leaving Dunvegan, say 40 miles above it.

From the entries in the journal on the following day, it does not appear
that they were that day, troubled with " strong current " or current
worth mentioning. On the fourth day, the entry is " current
strong," and yet this day, it would appear from the numerous beaver

lodges seen on the way, that the river was not so bad ; and in fact all day and all night, as they heard from the plunging of the beaver—it was beaver-flat, beaver country there. On the day, after that, without any further reference to current, save that it was not so strong, they arrived at the Portage at 5 p.m. But this Portage, be it remarked, is not of the canoes, which still keep to the river, and in so far as appears from the Journal, never left water till carried from McLeod's Lake, far on the other side of the Rocky Mountains, to the Fraser River at Fort St. James. The Portage was a long one of nine and a half, or say ten miles, to relieve the canoes, while they made a " horse-shoe " circuit of about 35 (thirty-five) miles as I estimate it.

The canoes accomplished the thirty-five miles, or even perhaps more, of bend in two days or less, and therefore there could not have been very much more difficulty than the average strong current. Moreover, in starting at the lower end of the portage, the only ascent, so far as appears from the Journal, was to the top of the bank of the river, and from that to the head of the portage all seems to have been level. My allowance, 6 feet per mile for rise at this bend, is, I really believe, in excess. On the following day there does not seem to have been any " strong current." On the day after that (7th September, exactly one month after the " cold, frosty morning " of Methy Portage, the height of land there), after " mounting the Grand Rapids, " *they actually, in canoe and with paddle, went through the Peace River Gap of the Rocky Mountains, skimming the waters*, stated by McKenzie to be here from 400 to 800 yards wide —lacustrine—on the west side of the Mountains, crossing the ridge, with paddle—" *à la nage*." So much for the " strong current, " in so far as it had to be traced all the way, as an element of measure of height and length of course.

As to current as a measure of height, I would here give the following extract from Russell again, because he is the author most in hand, and accessible to general readers.

Page 74.—" At low water the Peace River does not exceed a quarter of a mile in breadth below the Falls. At the Falls it is 400 yards. Its width up to the Rocky Mountains thus continues much the same, sometimes attaining 800 yards. *It has much less current than the Saskatchewan.* As to the current of the Saskatchewan, we find in page 64. " Captain Blackiston gives the average descent of the Saskatchewan from Edmonton to Lake Winnipeg at *one foot four inches to the mile.* To the foot of Cedar Lake it would be one foot three inches, the same as the descent of the Rhine from Strasbourg to the sea."

" Above this (the Rapids at or above the Forks) for the distance of 280 miles further up, to Edmonton, the ascent per mile is very much less than in the lower part of the river. It is estimated by Mr. Thompson, who surveyed it, as being from six to nine inches per mile, and for a hundred and eighty miles further up, to Edmonton, at two feet a mile, less than half the rate of the Rhone from Avignon to the sea. From Edmonton to within forty-three miles of Rocky Mountain House. Thompson states the ascent to be four feet per mile." My table of relative heights and distances will show how I apply these measures.

NOTE LVI.

" *A cross or two on the beach.*"—It has ever been the custom in the North, to mark all Christian burials with a cross on some conspicuous point near where the dead lie buried by the shore, or where death from drowning or otherwise occurred. In such cases there is no question of creed. The brotherhood of peril in those wilds makes *all* of one creed in such matters. When, in the " stilly silence " of the woods—that solemnity which ever, in some degree and varied aspect, strikes the human heart when moving in the primeval grandeurs of nature—those speaking monuments of our humanity suddenly catch the eye, they touch indeed the heart of common sympathy ; for, ever, it was some fine, brave fellow in the battle of life, and, perhaps, in the effort to save his fellows in peril, or working hard, that died there.

NOTE LVII.

" *Had a glance of the Rocky Mountains.*"—The point-view point, viz., from the lower end of the portage, spoken of in the Journal, is about seventy-five miles from the " Forks " of the Finlay branch (canoed in less than two days), and which Forks are beyond—considerably beyond, I take it—the ridge line of the Rocky Mountains, both these streams being entirely on the west or Pacific side of the Rocky Mountains. The gap in the mountains is, I have somewhere read, one of about " ninety miles," but that, evidently, is an exaggeration. I infer, from the Journal, that it is at least some miles in width, the very stream flowing through it, being, at the line of pass, from " 400 to 800 yards wide," as Sir Alexander McKenzie says, and with fine dry beaches and prairies, as Mr. McDonald reports.

Note LVIII.

" *The mountains, this afternoon, assume a stupendous appearance, snow on summit of several of them.*"—The " snow line," *i.e.*, line of perpetual snow in this latitude.   This latitude I place at 56° 18′ N.— a mere predicate, however, for I am not aware of any observation having been made to determine this interesting spot.   Possibly, Thompson may have done so. The nearest determined point is Dunvegan, given at 56° 6′, (by Colonel Lefroy.)   The next nearest is that of Cape Onmaney, the extreme southern point of King George III. Island, which is given in the naviga- tion tables, (Norie's), at 56° 10′.   The extreme northern point of Queen Charlotte Island, or rather an islet at the N. point called Langara Island, is also a relative point for estimate.   Langara, called also North Island, is stated at 54° 20′ N.   I give these points here, for I may have occasion hereafter to allude to them, at least to the latter, in relation to another branch of this subject of passage to the Pacific.

The longitude of this River Pass of the Range, I put at 122° 20′ W., about ninety miles within British Columbia.   As to what is the precise " snow line " at any particular latitude, there is no absolute rule, but merely a general one.   This is well illustrated by observations on this subject on and about the Himmalaya Range, as given by Humboldt in his work, "Aspects of Nature."   See note 10 in his annotations and ad- ditions, near end of note.   " From the data hitherto collected," he says, giving amongst others the observations of Captain Gerard—" It would " follow that we may take the lower limit of perpetual snow on the " *northern* side of the Himalaya at about 16,600 feet, (English feet) ; whilst on the *southern* declivity, the snow line *sinks* to about " 13,000 feet."   The italicization is my own.   The remarkable phenomenon is accounted for by the immense radiation of the vast Thibetian Plain.   We have a " Thibetian Plain " also, in those latitudes and meridians, and it, no doubt, has, in some measure, the same effect.   But besides that, the Northern Himalaya slope is comparatively sunless, while our Himalaya is blessed with the Phœbus kiss, full half the live long day.   On the other side of the range also, the border, broad, is plateau, in character very like the Thibetian Plain of open meadow, and only partially wooded, and of considerable radiating force.   But besides that, and more effectually and indisputably, is the melting agency of those warm vapours which the course and dash of the great Pacific Gulf Stream, that boundless, un- fathomed, but well known great " Black River " of the Japanese record, which, from the Torrid Zone, sweeping northwards along their eastern coasts, dashes through the Aleutian Archipelago, and bathes our north-western coasts with a heat force which it is hard for us of the east to estimate. From the authority at my elbow, (Humboldt, and there is no higher in his way), let me give an instance in exemplification. In his Note 18, he gives a comparative table of mean annual temperature :—

Sitka.—Lat. 57° 3′ ; Long. 136° 16′ W.

   Mean temp., 45° 5′, viz., Winter, 33° 4 ; Summer, 53°, Fahr.

"Fort George."—(Mouth of Columbia.)   Lat. 47°⊲ 18′, long. 122° 58.

   Mean (fahr.) 50° 3, Winter 37° 9, Summer 60°.

Geneva.—Lat. 46° 12, (Alt 1,298 E. f.), mean 49° 8, Winter 33° 6, summer 63° 5.

Fort Snelling.—Say now St. Paul, Mississippi.   Lat. 44° 53, mean Winter temp., 15° 9 Fahr.

Halifax.—Mean temp. 43° 5, viz., Winter 24° 2, Summer 63°.

Paris.—Mean temp. 51° 6, Winter 37° 8, Summer 64° 6.

New York.—Mean temp. 52° 5, Winter 32° 2 Summer 73°.

Gottenburg.—Lat. 57° 41, Mean 46° 4, Winter 31° 5, Summer 62°⊲ 4.

I give these figures to indicate, by comparison, what our British Columbia coast climate is, and to show that on the west side of the Rocky Mountains in the parallels in question, as well as the East there are natural causes for raising—and raising not a little—our snow line, at the view point Mr. McDonald speaks from. According to ordinary rule the " snow line " at 56° 18, or even 57°, should be about 4,000 feet or even less. I would be inclined to put it at 4,500, a maximum, especially as they appeared " stupendous " to Mr. McDonald's eyes ; and I know he was *truth itself,* as well as honor, and not given to exaggeration in any thing, and certainly not in depicting nature. A Highlander, bred and born himself (a McDonald of *Glencoe*—a name he gave to his place in Canada), he knew well what a mountain was, and would never have called mountains " stupendous," unless they really were so as he saw them then and there, and with his practiced eye, measured them from his foot. The foot in the pass was *low*, the objective snow summit was high, hence the " stupendous." Ben Nevis, (near Glencoe), of Scotland is, if I remem-ber aright, something approaching 5,000 feet in height, and yet though, almost touching the 57° of N. L., he always doffs his winter cap. Mr. McDonald, nor no Scotchman worthy the name, would call any thing much less, a " stupendous mountain."

Still, it cannot well be assumed that the Mountains so seen were of exceeding great height. At some distance from the mouth of the McKenzie River, at a point about 64° N.L. where the River, in its westerly trending strikes the foot of the Rocky Mountains, a spot referred to by Sir Alexander McKenzie, as "the hill by the river side," and which being easy, he ascended, the Rocky Mountains have run down to hills, *snowless even within the Arctic Circle* during the brief Arctic summer. On the other hand, to the south of the Peace River Pass, the ridge rises, till at the Athabasca Pass, in the Peaks of Mts. Brown and Hooker, about 300 miles South, it caluminates at a height of over sixteen thousand feet, the Pass there, being, as I thought, probably about 10,000 feet, but which has since been generally stated—on what authority I know not— at 7,000 feet above the sea. Intermediate, occurs the Yellow Head Pass, ascertained by measurement to be only 3,760 feet above the sea. No heights about this Pass except one, estimated at 7,000 feet, have been measured, so far as I am aware, although in the present survey for a Canadian Pacific Railway, there may have been something done in that way. The Yellow Head Pass is only about a hundred miles north of the Athabasca one. From the Yellow Head to the Peace River is a distance of about two hundred miles. The slope all along is most marked, and it extends till lost in that Arctic Coast, about 70° N. L., in which so flat is the land and immediate sea bed, that as Simpson (Thomas) reports, they had at places to keep three or four miles off shore to find water enough, say two feet or so, for their little light coasting boats. But it is not only the Ridge that thus slopes, but its bases do so, from the "Missouri Plateau," some four thousand feet above the sea, to the flats of the Polar Oblate. This apicial height, transverse to the Rocky Ridge, was I take it, the ideal 49° N.L.—our American boundary of 1818. It gave us all the Northern *Slope*. There was in that, a recognition of the geographical fact, that there was such a *slope*, and such *definite natural aoundary*.

Since 1818 the whole field, our's as well as the American, has been been traversed in different directions, in instrumental survey, sufficiently at least to prove the correctness of such geodesy.

Not incompatible with it, but in perfect accord, do we find the fact, that on that slope, at this lower point, the Peace River Pass, a navigable water course, five hundred miles nearer the flattened Arctic—has lowered to *less than eighteen hundred feet above the sea.*

"Less" than eighteen hundred feet above the sea! It will be asked, Yes, I say so, and say so on facts, which, as best was possible within my limited means and power, I have endeavoured to bring out, and in a way array, to prove (in so far as is possible at present) the "astounding fact," that we have such grand and golden gateway to the land Columbus sought, but reached not.

The figures are these :—-

	Feet.
Lake Athabasca, above Sea	600
,, ,, to Dunvegan	310
Rocky Mountain House above Dunvegan, say 140 m''es with rise of 3 feet per mile	420
Head of Portage from Rocky Mtn. House, say 35 miles by river, at 6 feet per mile	210
Pass (Ridge Line at River. say 70 miles from Head of Portage), at 3 feet per m'le	210
Total height of Pass above the sea	1,750

From such a point —one so low—those " hoary summits " (not old in story yet however,) snow-capped in *September,* may have well appeared somewhat " stupendous" even to our friend from Ben Nevis, and still be not over 4,000 feet or so. Sir Alexander McKenzie estimated (guessed) the mountain summit here in view, at 1,500 feet from the river.   That does not disprove what is advanced as to the height of the Pass : and as snow on *7th September* is quite possible on such height in that high latitnde, as a month---exactly a month before that—at about the same height at Methy Portage, the " cold *frosty* morning " occurred, there is no reason to believe that 1,500 feet or even double that above the river, there, is within " snow line " *i.e., line of perpetual* snow of that locality.

But further—-This subject of " snow-line," and the great question of— to use a Germanism—Rocky-Mountain-Snow-Railway-Difficulty, suggests an observation or two from me, from the special knowledge and sources of knowledge I happen to have on the subject.

The Athabasca Pass already alluded to, and which was used in my time in that region, viz., 1822 to 1826, was considered impassable even in *July,* on account of the *snow.* I went through it in early November, however.   In my father's journal of his journey from Kamloops (Thompson River) to Fort Vancouver (Columbia River), and thence to Edmonton across the Mountain, I find from special entry (a memo.) in it that he was to make special enquiry of one, " Jacques Finlay " as to the possibility of crossing the mountain by the Rocky Mountain Portage in July.   What the difficulty was, is not stated, but from the fact that the main difficulty at the time my father passed that way was *snow,* I presume that that was the difficulty.   On this subject, his journal runs thus :—" 1826, March 20th.—Started from Vancouver" [*i. e.* Fort

Vancouver on the Columbia River, and about 90 miles from its mouth, and then being the depôt for the whole Pacific trade of the Company ; from this point he started] "with the express for the east side" [*i.e.* east of the Rocky Mountains.] * * * " Left Spokan 17th April, and " arrived at the Rocky Mountains on the 27th. Put the boat, &c., i " security and started on the 28th, *but the snow was so deep* that we " were obliged to cut our leather trousers" [Note.—The long journeys on horseback necessitated leather trousers] " to make snow-shoes of. We " arrived on the east side the mountains on the 5th of May. Came to " Edmonton on the 17th."

There was, as appeared by the tree-tops, I have heard my father say, about " thirty feet of snow " under foot in the Pass then.

Before getting up to where the boat " was put in security "—a place called " Boat Encampment " by the Hudson's Bay people—there was considerable difficulty to the navigation on account of the snow, and much complaint especially from the difficulty, from that cause, of getting grass for the precious *first calves* which were then being taken by him to upper country of the Columbia, and as to which I may here remark *en passant*, he received the most favorable accounts some three years after, as appears by letter to him now before me. He had great difficulty in saving them, on the way, from the hungry clutches of the Indians at the portages, who wanted to make game of the dear things. Sir James Douglas may remember the occasion, for he also, from a simultaneous attack, had a narrow escape, when, according to my father's journal, " he owed his life to Douglas' quickness in taking off the cover of his gun, and the help of a gun muzzle or two from one or two others in the party." Douglas caught the first fellow of the attacking band in the act of drawing his bow, with arrow, at my father, behind his back.

Arriving at Okanagan (Fort Okanagan), on the Columbia, about 360 miles south of the latitude of the mouth of Fraser's River, and not half way from the sea to the Rocky Mountains, my father's entry in his journal is thus :—

" 1826, April, Thursday 6th.—I never saw so much snow at this " season of the year at this place."

" April, Sunday 23.—Started before daylight. Did not go far before " we found the Lake covered with ice from side to side. Broke our way " through with axe and poles."

" Monday, 24.—Snow and ice pending over the water edge along the " river which makes it difficult for the men to haul upon the line."

[The Columbia here, and, in fact throughout the whole one thousand

miles, at least, of the fearful voyage from Fort Vancouver to " Boat
Encampment," especially at this season of the year, runs with all the
force of a mill sluice. It is nearly all "*Dalles*" (sluices) with falls, cascades,
bad rapids, whirlpools, *chutes,* and every variety of water danger, and
many are drowned in the river every year.]

" Tuesday, 25th.—Hard frost late night. The ice is still in the bays
" along the river.

" *Wednesday, 26th.*—Weather very cold. *Six feet of Snow along the
water edge.*" [Fortunately ! the calves had been left in good and greener
pastures at Fort Colville (about half way up) far below.] " Breakfasted
" below the Crooked Rapid. The men we have with us who used to pass
" here in Spring, say they never saw so much snow as there is this year.
" The ice is yet as it was in winter in some places. The river we passed
" over to-day had, at places, on its edge, ice and snow 10 feet high. "

" *Thursday, 27th.*—Hard frost last night. Arrived at Portage about
" noon, and put the following articles in cache, &c.

This was the head of their navigation. " Boat Encampment," and the
" Portage " was the mountain just before them, and fearfully steep with
its from ten to thirty feet of snow.

The next Pass is the Yellow Head, or " *Tete Jaune Cache*" Pass.
That, also, has its " snow difficulty," as some of our family and a Mrs.
Ross, snow stopped in November in passage across the Mountain,
(for women could not then travel, though the men and myself did), had
occasion to know, the winter they spent at Jasper's House—True the
House—a very small concern I believe—was snowed up to the very roof,
if not beyond, but all survived the difficulty, and found it to be not much
of a difficulty, for life at least. It (the Yellow Head Pass) is travelled
in winter. Spring soon burst the snow bond with immense power, and in
June, the Pass, beautifully flower spangled, was passable to all.

The next Pass is that of the Peace River. There, in mid-May, Sir
Alexander McKenzie passed, and then, not only was there not a vestige
of snow, nor much, if any worth mentioning, on the "stupendous heights"
of his fellow Mac of the Mountain Land. In some Journal—but so many
years ago seen, 1 cannot remember—at some post near there—probably Mc
Leod's Fort, which is the nearest, but is on the western side of the
Mountains—I have read that on the "*6th April,*" the " Spring birds were
singing about the Post," and Spring fully set in. The 10th May record
of McKenzie, as to the flush of the sweet early green of the foliage, and
bursting of blossom, confirms—from our experience, in Canada, of such
law of arboreal development—the 6th of April record, or jotting of

memory. It was possible : that is enough. We too have spring birds—birds singing early sometimes, and the winter there, or at the next Post at least, as I shall further on shew, is no longer than our's, but the contrary.

There is in fact no snow difficulty whatever at the Peace River Pass, not not even in mid-Winter, the threshold is ever clear as that of an open gateway, ever clean swept by every wind of heaven. It is the most magnificent gateway between the two "worlds" of this earth, and bears the isotherm of strongest human development. A great Territorial Road (with branches) direct to it, and there striking the centre of a gold region probably the richest in the world, would fast people the whole intervening ocean of wheat field.

NOTE LIX.

"*Finlay's Branch.*—" Finlay's Branch " is, in fact, the main stream It is nearly three hundred miles in length, or at least its source is, I estimate, about that distance by river course from the Pass. It winds round a huge peak at its source—a Peak, in a system of Peaks, it would appear, from which the following rivers, as from a common centre take their rise, viz. That great River called *Rivière aux Liards*, and also Mountain River, debouching into the McKenzie at Fort Simpson, after a course of about 800 miles : Secondly, the Skeena or Simpson's River, running westward into the Pacific, at the head of Observatory Inlet. It borders, in part of its course, the south eastern boundary of Alaska. The reports of gold on the Skeena are of the most glowing character. They are likely to be true ; for " Queen Charlotte Island " near its mouth, has been long, for more than fifty years, well known as rich in gold—only, the indomitable " Natives " were ever in the way, and are so still, I believe. The river is reported navigable for light boats a good many miles up, but I have no authentic information on this point, as the trade, at the time I speak of, and whose record is before me, was not conducted there along that way. Fort Connolly is on a Lake (Lake Connolly) where issues this important water-way, and yet that Post used to be furnished by goods dragged up stream, and carried overland, all the way from Vancouver near the mouth of the Columbia, via Okanagan, Kamloops, Fort Alexandria, Fort St. James.

Since writing the above, I have learnt that steamboat navigation, up this river, is established for nearly one hundred miles.

NOTE LX.

" *Peace River diminishing fast.*"—In Arrowsmith's map already alluded to, I find the stream which flows from the South, past McLeod's

Lake, within about ten or twelve miles of it, and with which it commu-
nicates by the "little creek" spoken of in the Journal entries for 11th
September, is called "Peace River." In the map, the Finlay Branch,
from a direction N.N.W. and the so-called Peace River from a direction
S.S.W. meet at a point which I take to be just beyond the line of ridge
of the Rocky Mountains, for it was in approaching this spot of junction
that Mr. McDonald, in the "afternoon" of the 7th, speaks of the Mountains "assuming a stupendous appearance," and as to the following morning the entry is thus : "Started late. At another grand rapid by seven,
"and at Finlay's Branch twenty minutes after." It may therefore be
fairly assumed, that on the evening of the 7th, the voyagers camped on
or very near to the ridge line of the Mountains, in the very heart and
centre of the Pass. From that point, they followed the Southern prong
of the very open fork of the great river, leaving it, at say, abouut 120
miles from the Finlay Forks. From this point to the very source of the
said Peace River, a little Lake about 75 miles S.E. from mouth of Black
Water Creek, and further up on the Western Slope of the Mountain, the
surface stratum is, I believe, *Silurian*. Three hundred and seventeen yards
from this source of the Peace River, springs a small branch of Fraser's
River, striking, after a course S.E. and then S.W. the main stream about
120 miles W.N.W. of the Yellow Head Pass.

NOTE LXI.

"*Remarkably small white fish.*"—That is, "remarkably small" in comparison with those which Mr. McDonald had seen on the east side of the
mountain, along the waters from there to Hudson's Bay, which is the
white fish region proper, and where, in fact, it is the staff of life. It is
unquestionably the finest fish, and best food for man in the world. I
have seen it of every shape and size from Canada (inclusive), to the Arctic
waters, and at certain places, not only *ex necessitate* but *ever*, with unpalled
gastronomy, lived on it. Its peculiarity is its fineness of fibre, and
gout, sui generis, and in the further northern lakes especially, its creamy
looking and most delicately tasted fat or fattiness. A five or six pound
fish, in good season—say late in the fall, roasted, and in roasting laved
("basted") in its own melting of fat, which is allowed to penetrate all
parts of the fish by cross cutting, ("barring"), the sides at about an inch
a part, is the most delicious thing to eat I know of. The operation of
cooking this dish for an Apicius, worthy of Attehawmeg, as performed in
the North, is simply by suspension, *per caput*, with a cord or string that
wont *burn too* easily—a strip of bark will do—before or beside the fire.

I have tried the fish in his favorite waters with the fly ; using, besides different trout flies, a white fly in imitation of the little white moth which the fish were said to feed on, and which, in whitefish lakes, as well as in lakes not characteristically so, I saw was greedily taken by some fish or other, but ever gently and without slightest show above water. All said that it was the white fish that was so fond of this white fly. An old whipper of " Scottish streams," (and I have ever prided myself on my " cast "—*in that* way at least), I felt pretty confident of taking a rise out of my friends :—I say friends, for the *Attehawmeg* is a thing of the " Good Spirit," and is no one's enemy. It was vain—ever vain—at all hours of night and day, and in all weathers, and in all shades of light, and darkness even, I never got a bite. It is, in fact, a " vegetable eating " fish, but it is certainly reported by writers who never were in the whitefish country, or at least not long enough to know its habit, to take not only bait, but even " stail bait " on set lines, and also at times the fly." As to the bait taking, I know this much, I have often fished with bait— and all kinds ; living, stale ; spinning and set ; and that, in lakes where whitefish abounded, but never got one.

Ichthyologically described, the Whitefish, *Attehawmeg*, in Indian, Cree); Latin *Coregonus Albus*, is of the " order " *Malacopterygii Abdominalis ;* Family, *Salmonideæ ;* Genus, *Coregonus*. As to species, we have three or four stated. I have seen them of different sizes, from half a pound to ten pounds and over. I know of no difference of species, but know they differ much in size according to water—the coldest having the best and largest.

Note LXII.

"*Encamped on a small prairie.*"—According to all accounts—and I have them direct from persons long living in the country, and one of them at least, born in it—the general features of the country in those latitudes, from the Rocky Mountains to near the coast, is a plateau of " open prairies, lakes, and extensive meadows." I am citing from a report from a friend and correspondent there, and which report, for public ends, was formally given by him to the then Governor of British Columbia, Sir James Douglas, and which was subsequently embodied in a printed pamphlet. There is wood also on this plateau. As Mr. McDonald's Journal here shows, when he speaks of a certain " point of the woods," " over very fine country."

Note LXIII.

"*Fort St. James.*"—Is situated in about 54° 25′ N. lat. and 123° 30′ W. long. ; distant in a direction W., say 30° S., eighty-three miles from

McLeod's Fort, according to the itinerary of Mr. McDonald, and about 150 miles in air line, south-west from the Peace River Pass, and is about the same distance from Pacific water at the head of Gardner's Inlet, wherein falls Gardner's River, a celebrated salmon stream, having its source quite close bye.

In the Trade, Fort St. James was the principal depot for the whole country north of the Forks of the Fraser, (Forks some little distance south, as stated in the Journal), up to the Russian (now American) boundary, and including the "Babine Country"—a highland of water issue to two oceans, viz., Artic and Pacific; to the former by the Peace River and *Rivière aux Liards*, and to the other, by the *Skeena*, or Simpson River, and Salmon River— not the little " Salmon River " mentioned in the Journal as crossed on the march, and which falls into the *Fraser* nor the Salmon River, (so named on the map), which strikes the Pacific a little south of Observatory Inlet.

I refer to all these *(salmon)* streams as being, probably, possible highways for man as well as for the salmon which are found in their source lakes, on the very plateau, now marched on. No salmon has ever been seen or known to top, in its leap, fourteen feet in any British Atlantic stream. Possibly the " Ekewan," (hereafter described), of our Pacific, may, in his special lithe and strength, do more, but certainly not more than a foot or two. These facts are measures, approximate at least, in the question or problem of feasibilities for railway or roadway of some kind from this same plateau to the ocean. In other words the grade of the salmon way is, it may be rudely assumed, a measure of feasibily for any road for travel or traffic, and for railway, under ordinary conditions. I express this opinion without the slightest pretention to being any authority on the subject, for I am not a civil engineer; and I say thus much, merely to give my reasons for giving such details in connection with this account of a canoe voyage, and salmon ways.

Note LXIV.

" He " (Chief Factor Connolly) " *left the Pacific on the 23red of June,* " *and we left Hudson's Bay on the 12th July.*"—" We are on now what " may be called the height of land which forms this part of the continent " of America; and it is singular to remark, that without any previous " appointment, we should arrive here within two hours of each other, &c."

Very remarkable certainly, is the coincidence, " and singular also," adds Mr. McDonald, " is the coincidence, that the salmon in its annual ascent " for spawning has just, last night, made its appearance." Fort St. James (marked in most maps) is about 150 (one hundred and fifty) miles, (as I said before, under a different head) in air line from Pacific tide water, and in an air line about 1,200 (twelve hundred) miles from Atlantic waters at York Factory.

In the routes travelled by the respective parties, the disparity in length is not so great, being respectively about 1,500 miles and about 2,500 miles. Governor Simpson was, as I have before said, ever the fastest of travellers in the North, and the whole of his "empire" was at his command, and bent to the work. Mr. Connolly, from the very fact of being selected for the task, (one ever most arduous, and dangerous to even life, then) of conducting the "brigade of supplies" into the country, from Vancouver to this point, and perhaps to Fort Connolly, shows that he must have been a man of great energy, and no "lagger by the way." I knew Mr. Connolly well, and so did many, still surviving, of his friends in Montreal, where, on his retirement, he lived a few years. For his present journey, he, also, had the full resources of the Hudson's Bay Company at his command. We have seen how Governor Simpson, in his flying bark, got along. With Mr. Connolly it was a little different. I know it well. For four years my father being in charge of the Thompson's River District, had to go every year to Fort Voncouver, and thence bring up, in boats, and on horseback the trade supplies for the whole of the country between the Rocky mountains and the Pacific from the Columbia River to the Russian boundary, and far beyond. The manner of transport was by boats to Okanagan, horses in bands of from 2 to 300 from there to Kamloops, and thence to Fort Alexandria by horse also, thence by canoe to Fort St. James. The most arduous part of the route was the voyage up the Columbia. The "horse" part also, was very arduous especially from Okanagan to Kamloops, the whole distance from Fort Vancouver to that point, being about a 1,000 miles, The Okanagan valley, of immense length, over 300 miles probably is a beautiful pasture country, and is supposed by some to have been at one time the bed of the Columbia River ; (an error from bad geography.) From it to Kamloops the track skirts, or I should say skirted—for I am speaking of more than forty years ago—the eastern base of that huge coast range which the Fraser gorge (canyon) penetrates, and through which range also, the Columbia works its devious way, with many a "*dalle*" *and fiercce cascade*, a frightful navigation, especially in those numerous whirlpools which no skill nor power of paddle at times could cope with, and to which the bold adventurers had ever and anon to give tribute of life.

On the Thompson River plains, all was plain sailing, but still the journey was hard and wearisome, for there were mountains in the way. Thus it was, that Mr. Connolly could only take three steps, as it were, to the other's five.

But here the question naturally arises, Why this long round-about from near the mouth of the Columbia, when the mouth of the Fraser is so much nearer, and when, moreover, within about 150 miles, there is tide-water, the Pacific? There *was then* a special reason for that, but we shall touch on it more fully hereafter on arrival at the coast.

Note LXV.

" *Height of land which forms this part of the continent of America.*

This is an important statement. It was uttered, and entered in the immediate presence of men who were the most competent, from personal knowledge and experience, and especially Mr. Connolly, (a leading chief of that Western trade) most competent, I say, to form an opinion as to the geography of the Country. Of course, it was not meant, that the spot where Fort St. James was built, and which is at the southern or lower end of a very long lake, probably forty or fifty miles long, was absolutely the highest spot, but that the plateau—a *summit* one—on which it is, is the highest land or region in that part of this continent. Both Mr. Douglas (Sir James) and Mr. Connolly, men who had travelled the country thoroughly, from extreme to extreme I may say, and Governor Simpson (Sir George) who also knew the Country—for he had been, it would seem, an " old trader in the adjoining Peace River District,"—heard, and perhaps themselves made, the statement : besides that, I find by my father's papers, that during at least four years before 1828, *Mr. McDonald* was one of the Clerks in charge of some of the Posts in the Thompson's River District, and in fact took my father's place at Kamloops, as Chief Trader in charge in 1826, when my father left on leave of absence, [which he enjoyed, by the way, by proceeding to the very arduous task of building and completing Norway House.]

The charge included the whole area of Thompson's River District, a map of which was made by Mr. McDonald himself, with much detail and wonderful correctness, as has been since found. The extent of the District at that time, before the Coast District, and New Caledonia District were portioned off, was from the Columbia River to the Arctic Ocean, and from the Rocky Mountains to the Pacific and Russian boundary, in the North West of which boundary, beyond the narrow strip, (from 10 to 30 miles in width) ending at 56 .40'—Mount St. Elias (over 17,000 feet in height) is a mark and corner stone, the line running thence

to the eastern point of Beaufort Bay, on the Arctic Shore, along the
meridian of 131 .30′ W. In this large field there were several posts ; in
fact it was, in every respect, the largest, and most important district in
the whole vast area of the trade of the Company, no other district, (save
York Factory, with its special staff,) having more than three Clerks,
besides the Chief Factor or Chief Trader in charge, while this one had, in
1826, as I find by minutes of Council at Norway House, no less than
eleven. At the head of this list is Mr. McDonald, and it was—it is reasonable to assume—from *his special knowledge of the Country*, that he was
selected by the Governor to be his *guide* as well as companion. His
opinion, therefore, as well as that of the others just mentioned, is entitled
to special credit in such matter. And yet we know, from the very Journal
now before us, that the boasted " height of land " could have been no
higher—certainly not an hundred feet higher—than the Peace River
Pass. The proof is in this :

  From McLeod's Fort, which as before remarked, is on the west side of
the Rocky Mounains, to Fort St. James, is for the greater part of the
way, a down hill march. The itinerary indicates this ; for on the second
day after leaving McLeod's Fort, they came not only on little lakes
(indicative of a *low* rolling, flattish region) which they could, and did cir-
cumambulate, but on waters which they had to cross on rafts. Had these
been mountain or rapid streams on that height, there would have been no
need nor use for " rafts." One of the crossings in that way, viz., the one
that took them " three hours " was certainly that of a lake. They crossed
one unmistakeable river however, viz., that Salmon River which taking its
rise a little east of Stuart's Lake, flows into the Fraser River, in a general direction S.S.E. interposing its valley and watershed between Mc
Leod's Fort and Fort St. James, The watershed on that particular part
of the march, seems therefore to have been Southerly, with a slight trending to the East, and yet a few hours before that, before reaching the rim
of the McLeod Lake basin, a basin whose inflow is *from* the west and
south, the " lay of the land " was quite different. There could be no
better evidence of the *general* flatness of the region, than such diversity
of water-flow. In the account of the march, there is no *mention of any
ascent or descent*, until the triumphal entry *down* that memorable Hill,
into the Fort at its base. The Country marched over, and that by men
carrying big canoes—a most trying load, on acclivity or declivity—was in
fact, as appears by the " good time " made in the " portage," plain, smooth,
level, and easy for march as a parade ground. As to the height of McLeod's
Fort above that of the Pass, I judge it from the Canoe course—as so per-

fectly and graphically given in the journal—about 150 feet.

Starting from McLeod's Lake (which is fed by rivulets from the west and south, as before said, from a mere gentle uprise of the plateau, culminating about twenty miles from the lake) the march must have been on an up-slope ; but so gentle as not to call for remark, and the journal speaks as if all were smooth and level. In fact from the Rocky Mountain Ridge—*Silurian* to the very top—to the surf-beaten cliffs of the " Coast Range," so called, is a plateau of little variation from a perfect level, and of just sufficient " roll " or swell here and there, to give current to the abounding waters from the clouds, and to irrigate more beneficially, by a thousand rills as it were, the whole thirsty plain, with its lovely alternate of meadow, wood and prario, and to fill its fish teeming lakes.

The height of Fort St. James above the sea, I put at 1,800 feet, say fifty feet higher than the Pass. Measured from the Pacific level, three feet per mile (true measure I believe) to the six hundred miles or about that of Fraser River from Tide to Fort St. James, also gives precisely that height. For detail, see Itinerary. Between the Pass therefore, and the Pacific, there is a higher height, but on the most careful calculation I can make, it does not exceed 150 feet, due west, or nearly so, to the head of Gardner's R. or Salmon R. (West) : or in a line more northerly, say direct to Naas Harbour, Observatory Inlet, a maximum of 200 feet above the Pass.

Before leaving this interesting spot, the most northerly of " British Capitals," it may be well to answer, as best we can, the reasonable enquiry—What is the climate of that place and country ? What, its resources for human existance, or happiness?. My answer is—That remains to be, not found, but ascertained in their measure :—Such resources exist there largely.   The native there—a guage, in some decree, of economic value of a country—is no weakling of the genus *homo*, but a sturdy, " bumptious " sort of fellow ; not unlike the Waganda, and other such high living peoples of the Nile Upper Plateaux that Speke, in his book, speaks of.   Of the *Northern* part of British Columbia we—disgracefully —know little or nothing, save enough, perhaps, to make us feel, (I hope so at least, and it is this makes me now, hurriedly, write) that we *should* know more.   Surely, it is not, that the men of the South of British Columbia, who hold present rule, are afraid to open to public view, the grand middle and North of the magnificent country in their trust ! The present Session of our Dominion Parliament ; the drift of political influence on this head, may, &c.—But of that, more anon. To come back, however to this point of *our knowledge* of Northern British Columbia. On it, I dont

know exactly what to say :—I feel a little strongly on the subject, and the
direction of that feeling is adverse to those, who by their fair effort, nearer
home, have in some measure, won commendation. " To whip a willing
horse," is ever cruel, and I, for one—thank God—can never do it. Well
done, good and faithful ! should ever come ready to the lips. There is no
spur, like, encouragement of that kind. Well! as to this point, I repeat, I
dont know what to say, and shall for the nonce, borrow the words of the
" Chief Commissioner of Lands and Works in British Columbia," in his
report of 1867 or about then, an as given us by Harvey (page 7.)   They
run thus ; " *By far the greater part of the Colony is in fact entirely un-*
explored."   But let me give the whole sentence from Harvey's admirable
compilation—" Besides the valley of the lower Fraser, and the fine valley
" of the Chilcotin (the Chilcotin traverses the *middle* of British Columbia.)
" The bulk of the land available for agricultural or pastoral purposes is
" probably situated on the *high plateau* between the Cascades and the
" foot of the western slopes of the Rocky Mountains, but owing to the
broken character " [but that does not apply to our present higher latitude
at Fort St. James] " of its surface, and the heavy growth of forest trees
" and underbrush, the task of exploration is difficult, and the Chief Commissioner of Lands and Works reports that ' by far the greater part of
this Colony is, entirely unexplored'."   That " Chief Commissioner," if I
mistake not, is now the Governor, or Lieutenant Governor rather, of British
Columbia. Surely, *he* is to be believed !. But looking for some " Chief
Commissioner," of some older and more enlightened time—more enlightened as to the subject in hand—I find one worthy of equal credit—I
mean old Chief Factor Harmon—Daniel Williams Harmon, whose name
in the list of Chief Factors and Chief Traders, I find, beside those of my
grandfather and father in the original Deed Poll of Coalition of the two
Fur Companies, by which, as before stated the old N. W. Co., became
merged in the H. B.—Mr Harmon, a pious " Green Mountain Boy,"
schooled in Vermont, took service in the North, and doing well and
bravely his work, was, it would seem, promoted to the charge of the
higher plateau now under consideration, and which he retained for *several*
years. He, on retirement, published his journals, and the frequency of
reference, to his work is evidence of its merit.   I never saw it, but in a
book popular and easily accessible, called " Frank Forester's Fish and
Fishing," by H. W. Herbert, in a Supplement including a chapter—a capital one—on " The Salmon of the Pacific Waters "—I find a long extract
of the Journal kept by Mr. Harmon, for several years, while in charge at
Fort St. James. I cannot well divide it, and as every subject touched on

in it, is of interest, I give the whole extract, or at least such parts as have a direct or immediately relative bearing on our theme.

Page 27, "1811, May 11—STUART'S LAKE. The ice in the lake broke up this afternoon. 22nd—We now take Trout in the lake, with set lines and hooks, in considerable numbers, but they are not of a good kind. It is perhaps a little remarkable, that Pike or Pickerel have never been found in any of the lakes and rivers on the west side of the Rocky Mountains."

"*August 2.* It is impossible at this season to take fish out of this lake or river. Unless the Salmon from the sea soon make their appearance, our condition will be deplorable.— 10th. Sent all our people to a small lake about twelve miles off, out of which the natives take small fish, much resembling Salmon in shape and flavour, but not more than six inches long. [Note by Ed. These are probably the young fry, technically called "Pink," or, more probably still, the "Smolt" (more advanced young) of the Salmon]. "They are said to be very palatable.— 22nd. One of the natives has caught a Salmon, which is joyful intelligence to us all, for we expect in a few days to have abundance. These fish visit, to a greater or less extent, all the rivers in this region, and form the principal dependence of the inhabitants as their means of subsistence, &c.

"*September, 2nd.*—We have now the common salmon in abundance. They weigh from five to seven pounds. There are also a few of a larger kind, which will weigh sixty or seventy pounds." [Note by Ed. This is by far the largest average of salmon size in the world. The largest fish I have heard or read of, as caught in the St. Lawrence Gulf Waters, was one of 40 lbs. caught with the "fly." Query. Who was the lucky fellow ? In several editions of Walton, mention is made of *one* that weighed seventy pounds : Pennant has noticed one of seventy-four pounds ; but the largest known, in the record of British or Atlantic waters, is the noble dame—the queen of the sea—a female salmon of *eighty-three pounds* bought and sold by Mr. Groves, Fishmonger, Bond Street, London, in 1821. This fish is described as being very thick, and of fine color, in flesh, and of excellent quality. It would be interesting to know if the Pacific could beat that. For my part, I never saw a Scotch salmon—and tens of thousands have I seen—that would run over 25 lbs. and in our little Canadian back lakes, have myself caught *trout* much larger.] Says Mr. Harmon, continuing his entries for this day— ' Both of them are very good when just taken out of the water ; but when dried, as they are by the Indians here by the heat of the sun, or in the smoke of a fire, they are not very palatable. When salted they are excellent. As soon as the salmon come into Stuart's Lake, they go in search of the rivers and brooks that fall into it, and these streams they ascend so far as there is water to enable them to swim ; and when they can proceed no further, they remain there and die. None were ever seen to descend these streams. They are found dead in such numbers, in some places, as to infect the atmosphere with a terrible stench for a considerable distance round."

" *October, 21st.*—We have now in our store twenty-five thousand salmon. Four in a day are allowed to each man. I have sent some of our people to take White Fish, Attihawmeg."

" *November, 16th.*—Our fishermen have returned to the Fort, and inform me they have taken seven thonsand White Fish. They weigh from three to four pounds, and were taken in nine nets of sixty fathoms each. *17th.* The lake froze over in the night."

" *1812. January, 20th.*—I have returnd from visiting five villages of the Nateotains." [Note by Ed. Tribe between Fraser's Lake and crest of the Cascade Range, at the head of the Salmon River, which strikes, at Hopkin's Point, the head of the northern arm (Douglas Channel or Canal) of Gardner's Inlet.] " built on a lake of that name, which gives origin to a river that falls into Gardner's Inlet. They contain about two thousand inhabitants, who subsist principally on Salmon and other small fish, and are well made and robust.

The Salmon of Lake Nateotain have small scales, while those of Stuart's Lake have none." [Note by Ed. The only solution of the apparent anomaly is that the Nateotain, or Nuteotum as I have seen it elsewhere spelt, salmon is a different kind, probably the powerful *Ekewan*—of which more anon, which had taken the short cut from the sea to the height, viâ the Salmon River.]

" *May, 23rd.—Stuart's Lake.*—This morning the natives caught a Sturgeon that would weigh about 250 pounds. We frequently see much larger ones, which we cannot take for want of nets sufficiently strong to hold them." [Note by Ed. They harpoon them in the lower Columbia, where they attain a length of fifteen feet, and weight of nine hundred pounds. Their favorite food there is that most oily of fish the "delicious" smelt called Oulachan.

" *August 15th.*—Salmon begins to come up the river. Few Salmon came up Stuart's River this fall, but we procured a sufficient quantity at Frazer's Lake and Stillas. These Lakes discharge their waters in Fraser's River, which is about fifty rods wide, and has a pretty strong current. The natives pass the greater part of the summer on a chain of small lakes, where they procure excellent White Fish, Trout and Carp ; but towards the latter part of August, they return to the banks of the river, in order to take dry salmon for their subsistence during the succeeding winter. [Note by Ed. Salmon fare is the hardest I know of on the teeth, as it wears down the whole tooth, enamel and all, and in fact in that way, not to speak of its pro-dyspeptic properties, it shortens life ; it is death to eat it, as well as life.]

" *1813. August 12th.*"—Salmon arrived.

" *1814. August 5th.*"—Salmon begin to come up the river. They are generally taken in considerable numbers until the latter part of September. For a month they come up in multitudes, and we can take any numbers we please."

" *September 20th.*—We have had but few Salmon this year. It is only every second year that they are numerous, the reason of which I am unable to assign."

" *1815. August, 13th.—Frazer's Lake.* Salmon begins to come up the river, which lights up joy in the countenances both of ourselves and the natives, for we had become nearly destitute of provisions."

" *1816. September 9th.*—Salmon begin to come up this river."

[Note by Ed. The variation of date of arrival is to be accounted for in some measure at least, by the state of the waters in the main stream, its force and height of flood, some places being impassible until the highest waters make back water enough at the falls to enable the fish to get over. It is in that way that on the Columbia, the Salmon get over the Kettle Falls, which at low water are at least twenty feet high, a height far beyond the leap of even a Columbia Salmon. What other cause of variation there may be I cannot say. Salmon like other migratory animals are said to have a *sixth* sense, to guide them in their erratic course of life, and there is no reason to suppose that those of the Pacific are wanting in it.

" *1817. August 6th. Stuart's Lake.*—Salmon arrived. In the month of of June, we took out of this lake twenty-one sturgeon, that were from eight to twelve feet in length. One of them measured twelve feet two inches from its extreme points, four feet eleven inches round the middle, and would weigh from five hundred and fifty to six hundred pounds."

In the above extracts I purposely cover *several* years. On the coast, there is an immense variety of fish, including Cod, (fine, large and abundant,) herring, halibut, haddock, pilchard, whiting, sturgeon, oulachan, oysters, &c.

The staple of the country is—or was then—Salmon. This ever most interesting of water-game is worth a little description even in these hurried pages. It is not every man that can catch a Salmon, and fewer still that catching with his hook, can "land" "him," but every body can eat of him, and he is an "institution."

There is no part of the world where they more abound than in northern Pacific Streams, and though Sir John Richardson in his immortal work on North American Animal Life, has given a list, and full ichthyological description of the *Salmonidœ* of the Pacific Waters, I feel assured that we don't know half enough about them. My old friend Mr. McDonald was always enthusiastic (like a true Highlander) on the subject, but he went strongly for "pot," and most ardently for "salting," *secundum artem*, and not killing "the thing" by smoking, and it was to his importunity and enforcement, that at his Post—Fort Langley—which commanded in trade, a vast extent of sea line, the business of salting for market was entered into by the Company, if I mistake not.

The different kinds given by Richardson, and Dr. Gairdner (who was in H. B. Co's Service in the Columbia) are the following: 1. A small kind called Q*uannich*, averaging about three or four pounds. Abundant in both Columbia and Fraser. 2. The *Queachts*, a little larger. 3. The *T'suppitch*, average, say ten pounds. 4. The *Quinnat*, the main Salmon of the country, averaging from ten to fifteen pounds, and running to forty. 5. The noble *Ekewan*, the largest and most formidably mouthed Salmo —a veritable *Salmo Ferox*—we have any account of. His average is thirty pounds, but he runs up to double that.

Salmon and Sturgeon.—"Albany Beef."—such were the *pièces de resistance*, with *entre-mêts* of small Attihawmeg and *Carp*, at the "St. James" of those times in New Caledonia! But was there no meat, no beef, mutton, venison, fowl, meat of some kind or other to be had, it may be asked? No, none whatever, save a chance duck or two, or rarer still a deer. As to beef raising there was no possibility *then* of taking beef stock to the place, as everything, not to the manor born, had to be carried by man and horse fifteen hundred miles in the heat of summer. It was not till 1826, that even in middle Columbia, the first calves were introduced, and hard work, yea hard sheer fighting my father had to take them there, as Sir James Douglas, (then a Clerk in the H. B. Co's Service,) who was with him, and was the means, by his watchfulness and quickness with his gun, of saving my father from the treacherous arrows of the Indians on one of the portages, may remember, and it was not till about ten years after that that my father with other Hudson's Bay people went into the Puget Sound Agricultural Association, throwing in freely his £500 Stg. subscription, just because *he knew* the country was one calling for the experiment of stock raising and farming. Quickly, the supply exceeded the demand, and the cattle were left to run wild, it is said. This was on the lower ground—the coast. On the higher grounds, now under consideration, the same exuberance of vegetation is not to be found, but for grazing, it is not a whit inferior. There is grass enough in the plateaux of British Columbia, to raise beef for all England, and tallow for all Russia, and it is just the country for *Canadian* farmers, who know—ever know how to grapple the "snow difficulty" in their own or any other country. Harmon says it was "May 11th" when the ice broke up in Stuart's Lake. That is no later than with us in similar lakes, *still* lakes and not large river-lakes, ever with a current. The winter at Fort St. James, is, I take it, no worse for farming or grazing, than that of Ontario in the average, with probably no more snow, and entailing little or no housing of cattle, perhaps. In fact it is reported that the snow varies in average depth, there, only from six to eighteen inches, and covers the ground only from January to March. It may be so in some seasons, I have no doubt. On the same winter line of climate on the east side, say the country immediately north of the Saskatchewan to the Athabasca valley, inclusive, the cattle and horses winter out in the open, and get fat, and even further north to the Peace River, and to the north of it, hundreds of miles in that low forest land which extends continuously *five hundred miles* north of Dunvegan and to the very summits of the hills of the Clear Water Valley—Methy Portage—the wood-buffaloes can, in midwinter, "sun," as Simpson describes the sight, "their fat sides," and show then and there, beef to make any beef eater's, or more exquisite still, any buffalo-meat eater's teeth water. A fine country truly, and very Canadian! At Fort Liard, Lat. 60°, beef is raised, and salted.

NOTE LXVI.

Carriers." Whence the origin of the name, I know not, unless it be from the fact that they were much employed by the Hudson's Bay Company, and also by the North-West Company in *Carrying*, in their Country, where horses were scarce, and navigation was much limited, and other means of transport were wanting. Like many others of these Western tribes of the Pacific Slope, this tribe bears in its physical and mental constitution, and in its customs, marked evidences of its Asiatic origin—To the ethnologist there can be no more interesting field than British Columbia, and what more, until 15th June, 1846, (date of Oregon Treaty, if I remember right) was the Columbia of Britain—The whole is a scattered Babel of Tongues, to be accounted for, only by the probability, that they were ac-

cidental, and detached castaways from the many lands on the other side
—Mother Asia—and thence, were hither borne by the winds and the great
" Gulf Stream," of the Pacific.   The subject is of much interest, and as
" *two thirds*," according to the statement of Sir George Simpson, before
the Common's Committee of 1857, of the Indian population of British
North America is on the *west* side of the Rocky Mountains—and it is the
most unruly in the British Empire—it is one which will soon, yea *at once*,
does, call for serious consideration and prompt and energetic action; and the
motion in the Commons, of Mr. Wallace, the Member for Vancouver's
Island, on the subject on the 19th inst., (April) is well timed, and much
called for.   As to who, or what are our brethern of those far, old wilds,
we have very much, in fact, the Public concerned, and even the Government itself, has very much to learn, and the sooner it is learnt the better.
Those sturdy fellows of our western coast, are, in limb, and heart, in
strength and bravery, like very Britons, and will not be driven.   They'll
kill, or fighting, die first in the defence of their homes—Even to this day
they have held, what is probably one of the richest spots on earth,
Queen Charlotte Island, against all comers, Her Majesty's Battle Ships
included.   One agent alone they succumb to, viz, the deadly "fire-water;"
plied as it is with murderous energy, and in a manner and to a degree
which calls most loudly for prevention on the part of the Government.
But to return to our " Carriers," the best explanation of them I have
come across is Mr. Thomas Simpson's Narrative, already, so often alluded
to.   He does so, in giving the origin and affinities of certain tribes in
the lower McKenzie River region, traversed by him—He thus speaks of
then :

" The Esquimaux inhabiting all the Arctic shores of America have
doubtless originally spread from Greenland, which was peopled from
Northern Europe, but their neighbours, the Loucheux, of McKenzie
River" [Note by Ed. A people comparatively tall, athletic and of
finer physiognomy than the Esquimaux,] " have a clear tradition that
that their ancestors migrated from the *westward*, and crossed an arm of
the sea.   The language of the latter is entirely different from that of the
other known tribes who possess the vast region to the northward of a
line drawn from Churchill or Hudson's Bay, across the Rocky Mountains,
to New Caledonia.   These, comprending the Chipewyans, the Copper
Indians, the Beaver Indians of Peace River, the Dog-ribs, the Hare
Indians of McKenzie River and Great Bear Lake, the Thecanies, Nahanies,
and Dahadinnehs of the Mountains, and the *Carriers of New Caledonia*,
all speak dialects of the same original tongue.   Next to them succeed the

Crees, speaking another *distinct* language, and occupying another great section of the continent, extending from Lesser Slave Lake through the woody country on the north side of the Saskatchewan River, by Lake Winnipeg to York Factory, and from thence round the shores of Hudson's and James' Bays. South of the fiftieth parallel, the circles of affinity contract, but are still easily traced. The *Carriers* of New Caledonia, like the people of Hindostan, used, till lately, to burn their dead ; a ceremony in which the widow of the deceased, though not sacrificed as in the latter country, was compelled to continue beating with her hands upon the breast of the corpse while it slowly consumed on the funeral pile, in which cruel duty she was often severely scorched."

Such is the text of Simpson, and evidently from the context, he had carefully and with much admiration, read on the subject, " that eloquent and philosophical historian " (as he calls him) " Dr. Robertson," " who," he remarks, "has all but demonstrated that America was first peopled from Asia by Behring's Strait—The only work on Ethnology which I have read throughout is " Pickering's Races of Men," but it is bare, and scarcely throws any light on this subject of North American Races, and I am ashamed to say, I have not read Professor Wilson's standard work on the subject—My own gatherings of information, the remembered familiar words of those who spent many years amongst those different peoples, have given me some little food for thought—thought that finds but confirmation in the authorities just referred to. Amongst these facts, I may mention the striking one of identification of Jewish Customs, such as a feast of their's, corresponding somewhat with that of the Pentecost of the Jews, and also the habit of circumcision ; and more striking still is the Shuswhap law—most rigidly followed— ot the duty of a brother to take, " to wife," the widow of a deceased brother. Any interference in such case is " death," as worse than murder, the latter being compensable while the other is not, but is a mortal offence. The *Lex talionis* also, among the tribes generally, may be considered as something more than mere natural law. I cannot at present affirm that cremation is, or was, amongst these tribes confined to the Carriers, but certainly Sutteeism, in the sacrifice to the dead by the widow, in modified degrees, and varying in manner according to exigencies of habitat and habit of life, is to be found not only among the Pacific Coast or Slope tribes, but even among several on this side of the Mountains, such as the Chipewyans, and Montagnais. There was also that inhuman custom, traceable I think to Rajpootana in mid-Hindostan, where, for ought I know it may exist to this day, of casting female infants to the limbo of nonentity, as too good, or too bad (as the

case may be in the dark maternal mind) to live. But it is not only in
the hotter part of India that that hideous custom obtained, but in the
furthest North, amongst the Tribes, *other* than the Esquimaux, frequenting the Arctic seaboard between the McKenzie River and Behring's
Straits. The Hudson's Bay Company have, wherever they have established themselves, abolished these and such like habits, and in this they
show what power, for good, they have won amongst those rude tribes.
Even cremation and the modified sutteeism of the Carriers (a mercurial
and "touchy" race) has felt their pruning hand. "Instead of being
burnt, the New Caledonian widow (till the custom was abolished by the
Company) was obliged to serve, as a slave, the relatives of her deceased
husband for a term of one, two, or three years, during which she wore
round her neck a small bag containing part of the bones or ashes of her
former husband ; at the end of the allotted term a feast was made, and
she was declared at liberty to cast off her weeds and wed again." *(Note
to page 160 of Simpson's Narrative—Thomas Simpson's.)*

Note LXVII.

"*The War on the Sea Coast.*"—It was always "war" on that sea coast.
From the taking and destruction of the Tontine, a ship of some 350 tons
if I remember right, by the natives of this dread sea coast, who at the
same time murdered her crew, save one, many years before 1828, [I think
it was about 1813] there had been, in fact, *chronic* war with the natives
thus far, viz., in that they resisted every attempt at settlement, even for
trade alone, amongst them. The Sea fed them, clothed them, and gave
them all they needed, and they did not care much for trade. Still a running trade with schooners, and at last a steamer, the brave little Beaver
with her indomitable engineer Moore—all honor to his name as the
proto-pioneer of steam propulsion in the Pacific !— was ever kept up by
the Hudson's Bay Company, and that at a heavy loss for some years.
They had to do so, else the Americans, who had got a footing in this
coasting trade, could never have been driven off, and they would in that
case, have secured that "fact actual, of actual possesion," which Mr. Daniel
Webster, as Secretary of State, in arriving at the Treaty of 1846, so
earnestly sought to establish, in order to wrench from us the *whole* of our
Pacific Dominion.

It was a single intelligent mind, Lord Loughborough, that in 1824-5,
when the Russian claim was advanced, saved us any Pacific coast at all.
So the story runs. As to the Oregon Treaty, that was, we now feel, a
tremendous blunder ; and the only consolation in it is, that it might have

been worse. San Juan we should have, and it is to be regretted in that instance, that for once at least, the supremacy of British law, as sceptred in the constable's baton—for we British were in actual possession of the farm there at the time, and had ever been so by the right of first settlement—was lowered to the bayonets of General Harney—to a Foreign Power ! !

Note LXVIII.

" *Tête Jaune's Cache.*"—" Our communication with the Saskatchawin, with the leather, is in this way." Hence called also, and in fact, by the Hudson's Bay Co's people, is generally called *The Leather Pass*. The communication is easy enough for light loads, and even invalids have been sent by that way to the East, as being the easiest course. The leather alluded to, is that required, and that very largely, for the carrying service throughout the Columbia and Thompson's River and New Caledonia Districts.

The Columbia route from the east over "Rocky Mountain Portage," or Athabasca Pass, did not admit of any loads, and nothing but the lightest of baggage was possible. All the goods and freight came by sea round Cape Horn to the Columbia. Three ships were kept on that service. Leather, i. e., the dressed moose and deer skin, being scarce on the west side of the Mountain, had to be brought from the east side, where it was abundant.

The distance of the Pass from this point in the itinerary, viz., the mouth of Stuart's River, is about 250 miles by the River, which from the Cache (about half way) takes a decidedly northerly course, flanking the Bald Mountains of Cariboo. The descent of the Fraser to the Cache is that of a Mountain torrent, and to this point has a fall, probably of two thousand feet from its lake in the Pass.

Note LXIX.

" *Kamloops.*"—In my father's reports, journals, papers and letters, the name is always spelt Kameloops. The name is not in the journal of Mr. McDonald, at least where it reports arrival at " the House," and if it were necessary to show that those old notes by the way were never made nor intended for publication, there could be no better internal evidence of the fact, than the manner of them. It may have been noted, that at several places along the way—and these important, such as Cumberland House, House *de l'Ile à la Crosse*, and even Norway House, the capital of the Hudson's Bay Company's Dominions, which he, in the jaunty humour of the moment on arrival, calls " Jack River House," because it is close to Jack River, Mr. McDonald merely alludes to the place, as a man would, in passing his own house on the way. "Arrived at the house." What house? says the stranger—*Our house* of course, and the *only* house there or within hundreds of miles of it, says Mr. McDonald, speaking as one of the Company of proprietors.

So here at Kamloops, where Mr. McDonald was at home, in a sense—for, as I have before intimated, he in 1826, succeeded my father here—the entry "arrive at *the* house" without naming it, is, under the circumstances, quite a natural expression, and in its place, quite intelligible to to me at least.

Kamloops was always the "capital" of the Thompson's River District. My father was in charge of the District from 1822 to 1826, and a troublesome and most arduous, as well as perilous charge it was, as his reports, or drafts of reports, and his correspondence to and fro—now before me show. I remember the old compact and well palisaded Fort, and the "stockades" a little distance off, large enough for three or four hundred horses, for the horse brigades for transport of "goods in" and "returns out" for the District, and for New Caledonia, generally numbered about two hundred and fifty horses. A beautiful sight was that horse brigade, with no broken hacks in the train, but every animal in his full beauty of form and color, and all so tractable!—more tractable than anything I know of in civilized life. The Arab and his steed. It is in such life, that this splendid gift of nature to man, is best appreciated. One carried me, riding alone, and guiding with but child hand, over the Rocky Mountain Portage.

The Country about Kamloops is hard to describe clearly to those who have not crossed the Mountain. A region, it is, of peculiarly grassed sand plain, with rocks generally black or dark to the eye, of every form and size, and with that ruggedness and sharpness of "cut," which their origin (volcanic) gave them, and which the weathering of time has not yet rounded off—an *Arabia Petrea* verdurized—such to my memory of over forty-five years ago, is the great Shuswhap Plain about Kamloops and along the track southwards. It extends a great way back, fully three degrees east of Kamloops, according to the M.S. hand map of that region ; to the north, including the "great Shuswhap Lake," it extends almost a degree of Latitude, and towards the south to the Okanagan Country ; the western limit being that inter-range of Mountains—that other inner wall of defence or offence—known as the "Snow Range," and whose fierce heights or huge abruptions at the sources of the North Thompson and North River, on the proposed line of Railway through the Yellow Head Pass are likely to give much, but it is to be hoped not fruitless trouble.

If there be a block in the way to a Pacific Railway in that parallel of latitude, it will be found there, a stretch of some forty or fifty miles from the *Cache* to the immediate northern watershed of Quesnel Lake. Further but very much further south, there are I believe, one or two known passes, for I see in the hand map made by Mr. McDonald, of that country, marks of Indian trails from the Shuswhap Lakes to the Columbia, at or near the Upper Dalles, and also from one of the lower Okanagan Lakes to the Columbia River, at Kettle Falls. The " Little Dalles," near which is the now celebrated Eagle Pass, which Mr. Moberly (Walter, I presume) has the honor of having lately discovered, is I believe a considerable distance, I cannot estimate how many miles further down (S) the Columbia than the Upper Dalles, and over two hundred and fifty above the Kettle Falls. [In the Columbia River—so crooked and irregular, it is difficult to estimate distance.] In that parallel, and two degrees north of it, the Rocky Mountains are not in ridge, but are massed, with Peaks, a congeries of vastest Rocky Mountains, a hundred and twenty miles in width, from ten thousand to 16,000 (sixteen thousand) feet in height. It is folly to speak of a railway through such a region. If a Pass through the Rocky Mountains, and the " Snow Range," can be found with any degree of directness from the East into the Shuswhap prairie flat—no finer road bed for railway—good and well !--for as to the 25 miles of Frasers's River Can(y)on, and the 75 miles of other hard " navigation," in or on the lower Thompson, and below the Forks, surely the Locomotive—*à terre*—can follow the birch canoe ! We are bound to make the shortest road possible from sea to sea. I have my own opinion as to the proper Pacific Terminus, but that is not the point or aim of this present writing. Giving the Journal in hand for *public information, at this juncture*, that in all I profess to do at present. As to the Railway, it is, I feel assured in good hands.

According to my father's old reports of this Fort, it would seem that there were seven tribes that traded at it, viz., 1. The " Shew-shapps." 2. The Cou-ta-mine. 3. The Si-mi-la-ca-meachs. 4. The Okanagan. 5. The Stat-lam-chu. 6. The Spa-chil-quah. 7. The Shin-poo. The character and other particulars of each is given. They agreed but in one thing, viz., to disagree amongst each other, and as all, except the Shin-poos (of the north branch of the Thompson) are, or were then " most insolent to strangers when in small parties," and quarrelsome, lazy, and bad in every way, it was difficult, exceedingly, to get along with them.

There is no doubt but that on the whole, the Columbian Native is a most intractable animal, with the exception, let me say, of our lively, chatty friends the Carriers, and the gentle Shuswhaps. As to the Shin-poos, a mountain race, a remnant of the " Snare Indians," my father in his report says, that there were but few of them (about 60 families] and that they did not come very regularly to the Fort.

In connection with the question of road ways through the mountains, Rocky and Snow Ranges—in the southern latitudes of British Columbia, it may be not out of place to remark, that even in my father's time in that region, there was a very strong impression in his mind at least (and he from his wanderings, sometimes with but a single Kayoose—a knightly race then in those wilds—throughout the whole country round about, was in a position best to judge in such matter) that a much more direct course could be found for communication between Kamloops and Rocky Mountain Portage, than that round the south east viâ Okanagan—one more direct even than the most northerly of the Indian trails towards the Columbia, marked in the hand sketch map already alluded to, and even further north considerably, say from fifty to a hundred miles north of Mr. Moberley's " Eagle Pass," and so far nearer, if not actually on the parallel of the " Rocky Mountain Portage." And further, he seemed to think that a little further north, Passes through *both ranges* might be found. I happen to have the draft of his report made to the Governor and Council, as to the tribes in his district, in Spring, 1823. On this point, I make the following extract from it. " This Tribe " (the Shinpoo) " inhabits the north branch of Fhompsons River. They are good beaver hunters, *and go sometimes to and even east of the Rocky Mountains* "———" *I had in view*"—he goes on to say—" to have one or two " men to accompany them all summer, so as to endeavour to " meet the Gentlemen " (that is to say the Express and Passengers " coming in by Rocky Mountain Portage) " coming to the Columbia " next fall, at the little House " (which I believe was at the east end of " the Portage) " which would be by far a nearer and more practicable " way of obtaining a knowledge of the country about the heads of the " Thompson and N. Branch, than by sending from the east side, as Mr. " Annance was, last summer : the Tribe not having come to the Fort " this Spring, prevents my sending with them."

Mr. Annance, an Officer (Chief Clerk) of special ability for such work, had been, I take it, sent in from the East, viz., by the Leather Pass, to explore the country about the " heads of Thompson's R. and the North Branch—and which Milton and Cheadle so boldly did. This is the country, viz., that between the Athabasca Pass and the Leather, or Yellow Head Pass, which I believe, repelled even Doctor Hector, who is said to have been the most energetic of the Imperial Band of Rocky Mountain explorers, sent out about thirteen years ago.

I have no knowledge of the result of our Pacific Railway Survey in that quarter. I hope it has succeeded, or will so.

Note LXX.

" The River had risen three feet during the night. The little rain we had could not have been the cause of this."

Probably Mr. McDonald did not make due allowance for the *very narrow escape* which they, as well as the united waters of the two great rivers (Fraser and Thompson's) then and there were having.

I have heard and read of a rise of twenty feet in an incredibly short time, in some of the narrow gorges of this Fraser Can(y)on.

Note LXXI.

Leaping Simpson's Falls, under overhanging cliffs of the narrowest gorge of Fraser's Canyon. A Terrific Plunge !

The feat was bold : without compare : and we may, in vain ransack all record, ancient or modern, of brave travel, to match the simple, graphic, thrilling story before us. There is evidently, no coloring in the statement ; the whole preamble of that Journal leads to the irresistible conclusion, that every word there is true, true. Sir George Simpson was one of those men who know not fear. Mr. McDonald, though less demonstrative, and ever a Gentleman of utmost suavity, and grace of spirit as well as of form and " moving," not only, like Sir George, knew not fear and cared not for danger where *duty* led, but would almost court it. The nearest parallel to this feat that I have read of, is the running of Escape Rapid in the Coppermine River, by Dease and Simpson, along with the debâcle of the early Spring flood. After describing the work of dragging their boats (24 feet keel, 6 feet beam, light and strong of Athabasca Lake timber,) from Great Bear Lake, over many miles of hilly rock, and accompanying the ice in its breaking up and passage down stream, until they were stopped by the state of the flood, at a certain bad place, the narrative continues (page 257) " Tired of delay, we resolved to start at all hazards an the 25th, and pushed out at eight in the morning. From Sir John Franklin's description of the lower part of the Coppermine, we anticipated a day of danger and excitement, nor were we disappointed. Franklin made his descent on the 15th July, when the river had fallen to its summer level, but we were swept down by the spring flood, now at its very height. The swollen and tumultuous stream was still strewed with loose ice, while the inaccessible banks were piled up with ponderous fragments. The day was bright and lovely, as we shot down rapid after rapid ; in many of which we had to pull for our lives, to keep out of the suction of the precipices, along whose base the breakers raged and foamed with overwhelming fury.

Shortly before noon we came in sight of Escape Rapid of Franklin, and a glance of the over hanging-cliffs told us that there was no alternative but to run down with full cargo. In an instant we were in the vortex ; and before we were aware, my boat was borne towards an isolated rock, which the boiling surge almost concealed. To clear it on the outside was no longer possible ; our only chance of safety was to run between it and the lofty eastern cliff. The word was passed, and every breath was hushed. A stream which dashed down upon us over the brow of the precipice more than a hundred feet in height, mingled with the spray that whirled upwards from the rapid, forming a terrific shower bath. The Pass was about eight feet wide, and the error of a single foot on either side, would have been instant destruction. As guided by Sinclair's consummate skill, the boat shot safely through those jaws of death, an involuntary cheer arose. Our next impulse was to turn round to view the fate of our comrades behind. They had profited by the peril we incurred, and kept without the treacherous rock in time. The waves were there higher, and for a while we lost sight of our friends. When they emerged, the first object visible was the bow-man disgorging part of an intrusive wave which he had swallowed, and looked half drowned. Mr. Dease afterwards told me that the spray, which completely enveloped them, formed a gorgeous rainbow around the boat."

Bold, no doubt, and well done ! But that was with a boat, and the water was merely a " rapid," and foreknown, and not an unknown fall, with back lick enough to swamp a boat, and certainly a canoe.

Note LXXII.

" *Fort Langley*."—Was the first Sea Port, and Sea Fort, in what is now British Columbia. It had just been begun, and Mr. McDonald completed it.

According to a census, most elaborately made, and a perfect thing of its kind, (and I may say so, as an old Census Commissioner), it would seem that the natives round about there, were very numerous. My estimate from the figures was, roughly, over 50,000 for the whole country, having at the same time the reported numbers from some of the interior Posts to guide me in the estimate. They have diminished much since. The next, and in fact only other Sea coast Establishment in those *parages*, save Victoria, (which was an after work) was the establishment of Fort

Simpson, in Observatory Inlet, near the Russian Boundary. Fort Simpson, as appears from letters from that quarter in my possession, was established in fear and trembling ; so " wicked " were the Indians there, as elsewhere an the coast they had ever been.

However, Captain Simpson who had charge of the Cudboro, (the Company's trading Schooner there) did his part so well, as to get a footing without fighting for it, and started a Fort.

These two Establishments, regularly and strongly served by the Schooner, and after that by the steamer Beaver, and for a while by both, soon drove off American opposition, and in *that fact, besides the inland enterprise of the Company, was the conquest, for Britain, of the British Columbia of to-day.*

As to the lower, if not more valuable Columbia, Fort George at the mouth of the Columbia, and, on its abandonment Fort Vancouver, established ninety miles further up, dominated the whole country to the west and south—the whole watershed of the Columbia—yea even California to San Francisco, then under our trade and hand. That we have lost all that magnificent land —a seat for Empire—is a thing of the past. Regretful ! But instructive in this ; viz., That knowing *now* in some measure, the value of what we have lost—have thrown away—we should hold well what we have left unto us. To sell inheritance for a mess of potage is certainly no British duty ; and if by accident, it has been done once, we feel assured it will never be so again. Our's be it now, but to realize the mythic prophecy of our Boadicea's ancient Bard, when with " burning words he spoke "—

> " Then, the progeny that springs,
>   From the forests of our land,
>   Armed with thunder, clad with wings,
>   Shall a *wider* world command."